VON DOOGAN

and...

Starring in

The Great AIR RACE

HOW THE BOOK WORKS

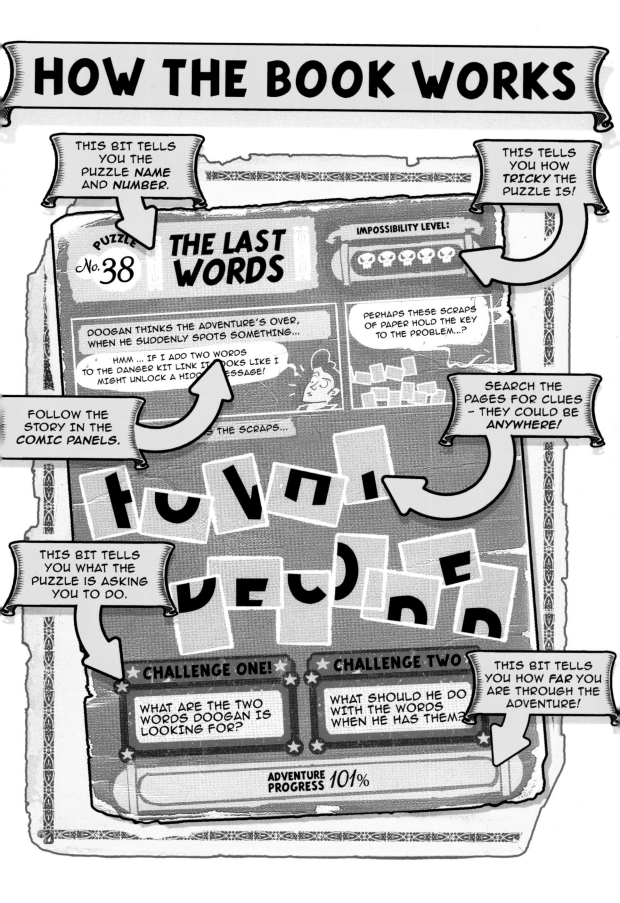

KEEN EYES AND A SHARP BRAIN ARE ALL THAT'S REQUIRED FOR MOST OF THE PUZZLES IN THIS BOOK. *HOWEVER*, THERE ARE A FEW CHALLENGES FOR WHICH YOU'LL *ALSO* NEED THE FOLLOWING...

★ ★ ★ EQUIPMENT CHECKLIST ★ ★ ★

- ★ A PENCIL ★ SCRAP PAPER
- ★ A PAIR OF SCISSORS

NEED HELP? THERE ARE **EXTRA CLUES** ON PAGE 42

STILL STUCK?! **SOLUTIONS** ON PAGE 44

FINALLY, THERE ARE SEVERAL *SPECIAL PUZZLES* THAT WILL INSTRUCT YOU TO USE *ITEMS* FROM

DOOGAN'S DANGER KIT
★ ★ ★ ★ ★ ★ ★ ★ ★ SEE PAGE 47 ★ ★ ★ ★ ★ ★ ★ ★ ★

GOT ALL THAT? THEN *YOU'RE READY!*

SANDWICH SECRET

IMPOSSIBILITY LEVEL:

THE WORLD FAMOUS DERRING-DOOER, *VON DOOGAN*, IS *BORED!* HAVING SOLD A RARE ARTEFACT FROM HIS *GOLDEN MONKEY* ADVENTURE FOR £22,000, OUR HERO IS GROWING *TIRED* OF THE EASY LIFE! LOUNGING LISTLESSLY IN THE TRANQUIL SURROUNDINGS OF THE *"WORLD ADVENTURERS' CLUB"*, THE DOOG FEELS *LOST*, AND HE LONGS FOR *DANGER* AND *EXCITEMENT*. BUT PERHAPS HIS *NEXT ESCAPADE* HAS *ALREADY BEGUN....!*

IT'S THE *SANDWICH CODE!* HELP DOOGAN DECYPHER THE MESSAGE BY COMPARING THE *SYMBOLS* IN THE *DANGER JOURNAL* BELOW TO *HIS VIEW* OF THE *ITEMS* ON THE TRAY...

Top Secret!
SANDWICH CODE

Decode the message in four steps in the order shown below:

STEP 1:
- BELOW THE
- BESIDE THE
- UNDER THE
- ABOVE THE
- NEXT TO THE
- IN THE
- ON THE LEFT OF
- ON THE RIGHT OF

STEP 2:
- RED
- BLUE
- YELLOW
- WHITE
- BLACK
- GREEN
- ORANGE
- PURPLE

STEP 3:
- RADIO
- CAKE
- DOG
- COAT
- LAMP
- BOOK
- VASE
- FRAME

STEP 4:
- BEHIND YOU
- BY THE CHAIR
- ON THE SHELF
- UNDER RUG
- ON THE WINDOW SILL

★ THE CHALLENGE! ★

1. WHAT DOES THE MESSAGE SAY?
2. IN WHICH LOCATION SHOULD DOOGAN LOOK?

ADVENTURE PROGRESS 3%

DOOGAN GRABS THE VASE AND GIVES IT A GOOD *SHAKE*. A BUNDLE OF *TOP SECRET* PAPERS DROP OUT...!

HMM ... BEFORE I CAN DECODE MESSAGE "A" I HAVE TO SOLVE THIS MAGIC SQUARE NUMBER PUZZLE...

TOP SECRET

– DESTINATION DECODER –
OPEN ONLY WHEN INSTRUCTED!
By order of A.R. INDUSTRIES *Limited*

DEAR *Von Doogan*,
PLEASE ACCEPT THIS INVITATION TO COMPETE IN *THE GREAT AIR RACE*, A ONCE IN A LIFETIME OPPORTUNITY. YOUR *FIRST CHALLENGE* IS TO DECODE MESSAGE "A" AND MESSAGE "B" CONTAINED WITHIN THIS PACKAGE.

PUZZLE 1

THE *MAGIC SQUARE* NUMBER PUZZLE.
Using the numbers 1 – 9 (using each number only *once*) write a number in each of the white circles so that all the *rows, columns,* and the two *diagonals* add up to *15* (see diagram below). The first three numbers have been filled in for you.

15
15
15
15
15
15 15 15

PUZZLE 2

MESSAGE A. Using The *Magic Square* as a reference, work out the *numeric value* of each symbol indicated by the *RED circles*.

Two are done for you.

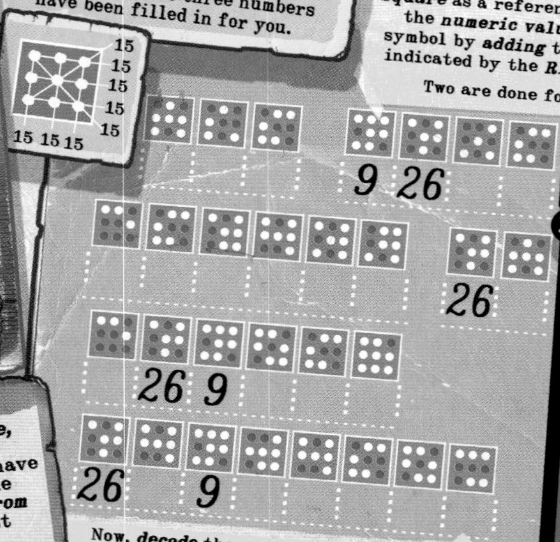

THE MAGIC SQUARE

9
3
6

9 26

26

26 9

26   9

Now, *decode* the numbers you've written using the following system 26=A, 25=B, 24=C, etc.

PUZZLE 3

MESSAGE B.
Draw *TWO SQUARES* inside the *Magic Square*, to divide it into *NINE* seperate sections, with one circle enclosed in each. Once you have solved this problem there will be one circle which is boxed inside a shape *different from all the others.* Use the number within that circle to complete this sentence:
"THE RACE STARTS ON THE _____ OF NOVEMBER"

★ THE ★
CHALLENGE!

SOLVE PUZZLES 1 – 3 IN ORDER, THEN ANSWER THESE QUESTIONS:
1. *WHERE WILL THE RACE START?*
2. *WHEN WILL IT BEGIN?*

ADVENTURE PROGRESS 6%

AEROPLANE EXPENSE

IMPOSSIBILITY LEVEL:

DOOGAN HEADS OUT, WITH **ADVENTURE** IN HIS HEART, AND **£22,000** IN HIS BACKPACK! HOWEVER, FINDING A **PLANE** AND A **CO-PILOT** PROVES **TRICKIER** THAN HE THOUGHT...

MONDAY MORNING...

SORRY, SON, WE ONLY HAVE PLANES SUITED FOR **SHORT HOPS**, NO **LONG DISTANCE** MODELS IN STOCK, I'M AFRAID!

HONEST JINGO'S **USED** AIRCRAFT

ED PLANE OR SALE 25,000

LION TAMER LOOKING FOR WORK

PILOTS ANT

MORE NEWS ON ASTEROID

ROBOTS

TUESDAY LUNCHTIME...

M. OUSTACHE PILOT ACADEMY

PAH! OUR PILOTS WILL ONLY FLY ON **LEGITIMATE** AIR ROUTES! THIS SECRET AIR RACE SOUNDS MIGHTY **SUSPICIOUS** TO ME!

AIRFORCE SURPLUS AUCTION SATURDAY

PIER 19 OUTH IDE OCE

NEW AIR ACE FILM

HUMAN CANNONBALL FOR HIRE

WEDNESDAY AFTERNOON...

LONG DISTANCE? YES, YES, WE HAVE MANY FINE AIRCRAFT IN STOCK, FEEL FREE TO BROWSE OUR CATALOGUE!

TOWN GAZETTE
LOCAL CIRCUS CLOSES AFTER WAVE OF THEFTS

Y PERFORM PT WITHOUT PLOYMENT

TWIN ENGINE £23,000

SHORT DISTANCE SOLO MODEL £15,000

LONG HAUL FLYER £30,000

LEARN TO FLY! (1 YEAR COURSE)

VISIT SUNNY JAVASU ISLAND

THURSDAY EVENING...

FOR SALE 22,500

HOP HARRIGAN'S FLYING SCHOOL

SORRY, WE DON'T HAVE ANY JUNIOR PILOTS WITH FULL LICENCES. CAN IT WAIT UNTIL THE **NEW YEAR**...?

AIR BATTLE MOVIE STAR APPEARING TONIGHT!

LIVE! THURSDAY ONLY!

THE BARLEY CIRCUS

FEATURING ABBEY "ACE" PONTOON DAREDEVIL PILOT! NCELLED

COME TO THE A.S. AUCTION FOR ROCK BOTTOM PRICES!

STRANSKI

IS TH EMP OF T ZOM QUE REA

FRIDAY NIGHT...

'SIGH' WHAT A WASH-OUT! SO MUCH FOR MY **BIG ADVENTURE!**

MORE COFFEE HERE PLEASE, AND MAKE IT SNAPPY! I HAVE A FLIGHT TO CATCH!

ROBOTICS PROFESSOR MISSING

BARLEY BLURB MOVIE STAR LEAVING!

ASTEROID ETTING LOSER

TODAY'S SPECIAL: BANANA AND CHOC MILKSHA

★ THE CHALLENGE! ★

EXAMINE THE PANELS ABOVE AND HELP DOOGAN FIND...
1. THE **NAME** AND **LOCATION** OF A CO-PILOT HE COULD APPROACH.
2. **WHERE** TO PICK UP A BARGAIN PLANE!

ADVENTURE PROGRESS *8%*

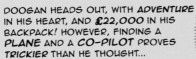

THE BIG COFFEE POT

DOOGAN'S SUSPICIONS ARE RIGHT, THE WAITRESS IS ABBEY "ACE" PONTOON...!

The Little Cafe

ANCIENT KINGDOM DISCOVER

I'LL MAKE YOU A DEAL, MR DOOGAN. PROVE TO ME YOU'RE A FIRST-CLASS PILOT BY SUCCESSFULLY NAVIGATING A POT OF COFFEE THROUGH THIS CAFÉ, AND I'LL JOIN YOUR CREW!

THE CHALLENGE!

1) You begin at the point marked **START** with enough coffee in your pot to pour **7 CUPS**.

2) Chose your route through the café to reach the **FINISH**. You can **ONLY** move in the direction of the arrows.

3) Each time you come to a table you must pour the number of coffees as indicated by the number on the table (-3 etc).

4) Each time you come to a filling station you may re-fuel your pot by the number of cups shown (+4 etc).

5) Keep a running total of how many cups worth of coffee you have in your pot. If you get to a table and you don't have enough coffee to pour **ALL** the cups, you **lose!**

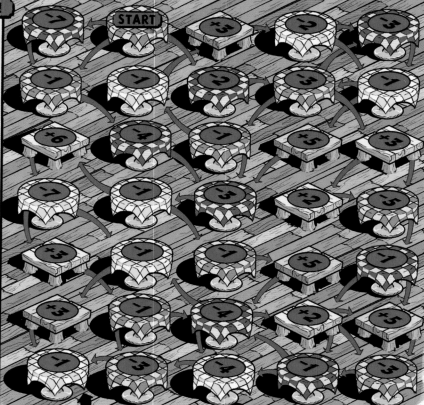

THE CHALLENGE!

HOW MANY CUPS OF COFFEE ARE LEFT IN THE POT AT THE *FINISH?*

ADVENTURE PROGRESS *11%*

PUZZLE No. 5

THE BIDDING WAR

IMPOSSIBILITY LEVEL:

WITH ABBEY ON BOARD, DOOGAN HEADS FOR THE *AIRFORCE SURPLUS AUCTION*, TO *BUY* AND *EQUIP* A SUITABLE AEROPLANE FOR THE RACE...

THE AUCTION!

THE AUCTIONEER CALLS OUT THE *RESERVE PRICE* AND THE BIDDING BEGINS. EACH RED PADDLE UPS THE TOTAL PRICE BY £1,250, GREEN BY £1,500 AND BLUE BY £1,750.

WHAT IS DOOGAN'S *WINNING BID?*

 NEXT UP, LOT NUMBER 113, A B17 FLYING FORTRESS.

 WHO WILL START THE BIDDING AT £4,150?

 GOING, GOING, GONE! SOLD TO THE GENT WITH THE QUIFF!

THE SUPPLIES!

DOOGAN STARTED WITH £22,000. TAKING INTO ACCOUNT WHAT HE SPENT IN THE AUCTION, AND THE £1,600 HE PAID TO HIRE ABBEY, CAN HE AFFORD TO GET *EVERYTHING* ON HIS SHOPPING LIST?

Hungry Arnold's Foodstuffs

Each hamper holds a **full day's** food for the stated number of people.

Basic Hamper (feeds 8)............£40
Large Hamper (feeds 20).........£60
Deluxe Hamper (feeds 40).......£100
Super Hamper (feeds 80)........£180
....£250
Monster Hamper
Atomic Hamper
Gargantuan Ha
Godzilla Hamp

RADIO SHED

LONG WAVE UNITS

"THE BIG RECEIVER" High quality build. Only.....................£40

"THE ZINGER" nest tubes. ly.......................£80

E MIGHTY BOX" quality build

SHORT WAVE UNITS

"THE LIL' YAPPER" Strong signals. Only.....................£120

"THE TUBE-A-TRON" Send and recieve! Only.....................£90

SHOPPING LIST

Food for 2 people for twenty days
2 Parachutes
A Shortwave radio
A full set of maps

AIRFORCE SURPLUS

ORDINANCE MAP BUNDLES

Atlantic Maps.....£10
Javasu islands...£12
Frozen Lands.....£13
Full set............£18
Deluxe set.........£40

OXYGEN TANKS

"Easy Breather" Fully articul

TWIN PARACHUTE SETS

"The Big Droppers"
Set only............£30
"The Safety Silks"
Set only............£60
"The Freefallers"
Set only............£90

★ THE CHALLENGE! ★

1. WHAT WAS DOOGAN'S WINNING BID AT THE AUCTION?
2. HOW MUCH DOES HE HAVE LEFT TO SPEND ON SUPPLIES?
3. WHICH 4 ITEMS SHOULD HE BUY?
4. HOW MUCH MONEY DOES HE HAVE LEFT?

ADVENTURE PROGRESS *14%*

TERRIFYING TAKE-OFF

IMPOSSIBILITY LEVEL:

THE ROAR OF MANY *POWERFUL* ENGINES, THE RUMBLE OF *GIANT* WHEELS ON CRACKED TARMAC, AND THE GREAT AIR RACE COMMENCES!

A PERFECT TAKE-OFF, ABBEY! BRAVO!

DON'T CELEBRATE YET! IT'S PRETTY *CROWDED* UP HERE ... WE'RE GOING TO NEED A HEAVY DOSE OF *LUCK* JUST TO CLEAR THE AIRFIELD!

TO COMPLETE THIS CHALLENGE YOU'LL NEED THE PLAYING PIECES FROM

DOOGAN'S DANGER KIT

Quick! GO TO PAGE 47

THE RULES!

A) Print and cut out the six playing pieces. These represent the *leading* five air racers, and Doogan. Alternatively, use coins instead, but mark one as THE DOOG!

B) Place DOOGAN on the spot marked with a "D" and the five racer pieces on the "X"s.

C) Each turn FIRST move *ALL FIVE RACER* pieces *ONE SPACE*, then move the DOOGAN piece *ONE SPACE*, obeying the rules below:

1) YOU choose the path DOOGAN takes, BUT he can ONLY move *STRAIGHT UP, STRAIGHT DOWN* or *DIRECTLY RIGHT,* and he CANNOT use the same space twice!

2) The other flyers ALWAYS move to the next space indicated by an ARROW.

-------- DOOGAN CRASHES *IF...* --------

He moves into a space occupied by one of the other flyers, OR one of the flyers moves into a space occupied by Doogan!

SAFE! 1

SAFE! 2

SAFE! 3

★ **THE CHALLENGE!** ★

WHICH OF THE "SAFE" SQUARES CAN DOOGAN REACH FIRST?

ADVENTURE PROGRESS 22%

PERILOUS PART SWAP

IMPOSSIBILITY LEVEL:

DOOGAN BREATHES A SIGH OF RELIEF, WHEN SUDDENLY, *CALAMITY!* A BURST OF TURBULANCE SENDS THE *THUNDERBOLT* CRASHING INTO THE PATH OF THE *ROYAL ROCKET...!*

TERRIFYING SECONDS PASS, AS THE TWO PLANES CRUNCH AGAINST EACH OTHER *MID-AIR!*

BOTH PILOTS *WRENCH* AT THEIR CONTROLS...

... AND WITH *BARELY MOMENTS TO SPARE* THEY PULL THE PLANES APART, BUT DOOGAN'S LANDING GEAR IS *WRECKED!*

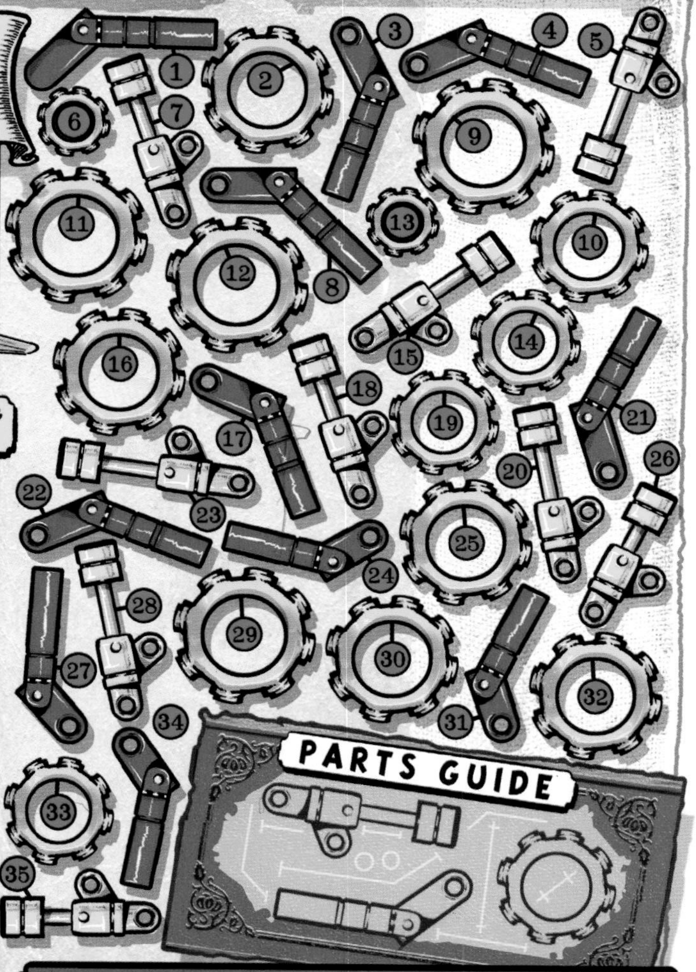

PARTS GUIDE

★ THE CHALLENGE! ★

THE DOOG SURVEYS THE DAMAGE. THERE ARE *THREE* MAIN PARTS THAT MUST BE REPLACED BY PIECES WITH *EXACTLY* THE SAME *SHAPE* AND *DIMENSIONS*. USING A *RULER* (OR A SCRAP OF PAPER ON WHICH TO MAKE MEASUREMENT MARKS) CAN YOU IDENTIFY THE *THREE PARTS* DOOGAN NEEDS?

ADVENTURE PROGRESS 24%

THE BIG CHOKE

THE FIRST LEG OF THE *GREAT AIR RACE* CONTINUES WITHOUT INCIDENT. AS DUSK APPROACHES, THE FLYERS LAND AT *CHECKPOINT BOBO...*

LEADER BOARD
By order of
A.R. INDUSTRIES
Limited

1ST – KLAUS
2ND – DOOGAN
3RD – WINGNUT
4TH – TOOLA
5TH – GOUDA
6TH – KARMANN
7TH – JAKOBS
8TH – MARLIN

* As recorded at Checkpoint Bobo.

THAT EVENING, EVERYONE *EXCEPT GOUDA* HEADS OUT TO THE LOCAL PILOTS' EATERY, *CAFÉ EGG.*

NEXT RIGHT
Open 'till Late!

WITH HIS STOMACH FULL OF *PIZZA* AND HIS HEAD FULL OF *AEROPLANES,* DOOGAN PREPARES TO LEAVE, WHEN *KLAUS* CRIES OUT...

POISON!

Mains Waiter:
" I ENTERED FROM THE **KITCHEN** AND HEADED FOR THE **BAR,** WHERE I **STOPPED** TO PICK UP SOME DRINKS. I THEN WALKED BETWEEN TABLES **ONE** AND **TWO** AND ON TO **FOUR** AND **FIVE.** I **STOPPED** AT TABLE **FIVE,** PICKED UP AN EMPTY GLASS, AND THEN I WALKED ON TO TABLE **SEVEN.** "

Times of **Klaus's** courses leaving bar/kitchen /dessert station:

Drinks: 7:30
Starter: 7:50
Main: 8:20
Dessert: 9:00

None of the pilots left the café during their meals except...

I WAS AWAY FROM MY TABLE FROM 7:25 TO 7:40.

JAKOBS!

Drinks Waiter:
" I ENTERED FROM THE **BAR** AND WENT STRAIGHT TO **WINDOW A,** WHICH I **STOPPED** TO OPEN. I THEN **STOPPED** AT TABLE **TWO** TO DROP OFF A DRINK BEFORE WALKING ON TO TABLE **SEVEN.** "

Starters Waiter
" I ENTERED FROM THE **KITCHEN** AND HEADED IN THE DIRECTION OF TABLE **SIX.** I **STOPPED** BY TABLE **ONE** TO ANSWER A QUESTION, AND THEN WALKED ON TO TABLE **SEVEN.**"

MAP OF CAFÉ EGG.

KITCHEN | BAR

1 2 A
3
4 5 B
6 7

DESSERT STATION

...and...

I WAS AWAY BETWEEN 7:45 AND 8:00.

DOOGAN!

Dessert Waiter:
" I CAME FROM THE **DESSERT STATION** AND STOPPED TO SERVE A BANANA PANCAKE TO TABLE **SIX.** I THEN CONTINUED ON TO TABLE **SEVEN.** "

The poison was fairly slow acting, so could have been given at any point during the meal...

➤ **KLAUS WAS ON 7!**

IMPORTANT: WHEN A WAITER STOPS AT **ANY** LOCATION, HE STANDS IN THE DOTTED AREA IN WHICH THAT LOCATION FALLS (BASED ALSO UPON THE DIRECTION HE WAS WALKING). DINERS ON **ANY** OF THE TABLES THAT **ALSO** FALL WITHIN THE DOTTED AREA CAN **TAMPER** WITH THE WAITER'S TRAY. EXAMPLE: IF THE WAITER STOPS AT TABLE 3, TABLES 4, 1 AND 3 CAN ALL TAMPER WITH HIS TRAY!

Some of the pilots went home before Klaus cried out at 9:30...

I LEFT AT 8:40 — **KARMANN**
I LEFT AT 8:00 — **JAKOBS**
I LEFT AT 8:30 — **TOOLA**
LIKEWISE! — **MARLIN**

Marlin sat at an even numbered table ✲ Toolah sat at the table directly left of Karmann ✲ Jakobs sat at the table directly above Klaus's ✲ Doogan's table number was one less than Klaus' ✲ Karmann sat at the table closest to window A ✲

★ THE CHALLENGE! ★
LOOKING AT THE INFO DOOGAN GATHERED, IT IS CLEAR THAT ONLY **ONE** OF THE PILOTS WHO ATE IN THE CAFÉ DID **NOT** HAVE AN OPPORTUNITY TO POISON KLAUS. **WHO WAS IT?**

ADVENTURE PROGRESS *27%*

THE DEADLY OVERSLEEP

IMPOSSIBILITY LEVEL:

KLAUS IS RUSHED TO HOSPITAL, AND THE REMAINING FLYERS RETIRE TO THEIR CABINS. THE NEXT MORNING, DOOGAN IS *AWAKENED* BY THE SOUND OF *AEROPLANES ROARING DOWN THE RUNWAY!*

HOLY TOMBOLAS! WHAT'S ALL THIS?!

OUR HERO'S ALARM CLOCK HAS BEEN TURNED OFF AND HE'S BEEN *BARRICADED* INTO HIS ROOM!

SUDDENLY, WISPS OF *SMOKE* COME SEEPING THROUGH THE WALLS...!

FIRE!

SKYLIGHT A: TOO HIGH TO REACH AND GLUED SHUT.

FRONT DOOR BARRED FROM THE OUTSIDE.

SKYLIGHT B: TOO HIGH TO REACH AND SCREWED SHUT.

SIDE DOOR BOLTED FROM THE OUTSIDE

WINDOW B: SCREWED SHUT FROM THE OUTSIDE.

TRAPDOOR: PADLOCKED AND BOLTED DOWN.

BACK DOOR GLUED SHUT AND LOCKED

WINDOW A: BARRED WITH PLANKS BOLTED DOWN.

★ THE CHALLENGE! ★

LOOK AROUND THE CABIN. WHICH EXIT CAN DOOGAN ESCAPE THROUGH? WHAT ITEMS SHOULD HE USE TO MAKE THIS POSSIBLE?

ADVENTURE PROGRESS 30%

SIX SCRAPS AND A MAP

DOOGAN *ESCAPES*, ONLY TO DISCOVER THAT THE SMOKE WAS *ACTUALLY COMING FROM THE HANGAR HOUSING THE THUNDERBOLT!*

QUICK! THE PLANE!

OH! DOOGAN ... THERE YOU ARE. I WAS JUST OUT BUYING US BREAKFAST WHEN I SAW THE SMOKE...

SAND

FORTUNATELY, ABBEY HAD MANAGED TO TAXI THE THUNDERBOLT TO SAFETY. THE *"SECRET WING"*, PILOTED BY *JAKE WINGNUT*, WASN'T SO LUCKY...

LOOKS LIKE I'M OUT OF THE RACE FOR *GOOD*, OLD CHUM!

DOOGAN!

WINGNUT!

THE REMAINING *FIVE FLYERS* ALL SEEM TO HAVE SET OFF *BEFORE* THE FIRE WAS SPOTTED, LEAVING THE DOOG IN *LAST PLACE*, WITH *NO IDEA OF THE NEXT CHECKPOINT DESTINATION!*

LOOK TO THE

WITH THE SKULLS.

IS NORTH-EAST OF

NORTH OF THE REEF

WEST OF THE RED ISLAND

YOUR GOAL

EAST OF THE ROCK

THE SHIPWRECK

YOUR DESTINATION.

YOUR GOAL IS

WITH THE LIGHTNING AND

NUMBERING NO MORE THAN

SOUTH OF THE ROCK

THE TREES

THREE.

YOUR DESTINATION IS

WITH THE SHARKS.

YOU WILL FIND

ARRANGE THE SCRAPS INTO A RECTANGLE THEN READ THE FULL MESSAGE!

★ THE CHALLENGE! ★

DOOGAN OPENS THE *DESTINATION DECODER* TO THE PAGE FOR *"CHECKPOINT WETFOOT"*. INSIDE ARE *SIX SCRAPS* OF PAPER AND A *MAP*. THE SCRAPS MUST BE ARRANGED INTO A *RECTANGLE (SEE DIAGRAM)* SO THAT THEIR MESSAGE, WHEN READ *IN FULL*, DIRECTS DOOGAN TO A LOCATION ON THE MAP. AT WHAT *COORDINATES (X / Y)* IS THE *CORRECT DESTINATION?* HINT – IT CAN BE ON DRY LAND OR IN THE SEA!

KEY:
REEF
WRECK
ROCK

DEATH ISLAND
SKULL ROCK

Y AXIS
5
4
3
2
1
A B C D E F
X AXIS

ADVENTURE PROGRESS 32%

PUZZLE No. 13 — MIXED MESSAGES

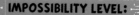

IMPOSSIBILITY LEVEL:

VON DOOGAN IS *BACK IN THE RACE!* THE THUNDERBOLT TAKES TO THE SKY!

RRROAR!

OUR HERO LEAVES ABBEY AT THE CONTROLS AND GOES TO THE *POWERFUL RADIO RECEIVER* IN THE BACK OF THE PLANE...

GOT TO PICK UP SOME *WEATHER REPORTS* FOR THE NEXT LEG OF THE JOURNEY!

THE DOOG STUMBLES ACROSS A *STRANGE BROADCAST,* ITS MESSAGE *ENCRYPTED* IN A MIXTURE OF CODES...

STPMETTABALA NOBALA SUABALALK DNABALA TUNGNIBALAW LUFSSECCUBALAS. REVEWOBALAH NOBALAV NAGOOBALAD DEPACSEBALA. EBALAH SIBALA NOBALA OBALAT SUBALA, KNIBALAHT EBALAW YABALAM DEEBALAN OBALAT EVOBALAM OBALAT NABALALP OWBALAT. TEBALAG SGNIBALAHT YDAEBALAR NOBALA EBALAHT TFARCRIABALA REIRRABALAC DNABALA IBALA LLIBALAW TCATNOBALAC UOBALAY NIAGABALA NIBALA OWBALAT SYABALAD.

DOOGAN'S DECODER

- **CODE TYPE 1:** Entire message written in reverse.
- **CODE TYPE 2:** Words in correct order, but each word spelt backwards.
- **CODE TYPE 3:** First and last letters of each word swapped.
- **CODE TYPE 4:** Only every third word is part of the actual message.
- **CODE TYPE 5:** Using the system A=26, B=25, C=24 etc, replace each letter in your code message with its corresponding number.
- **CODE TYPE 6:** Put the letters "alab" before the first vowel of each word. Example: "Feet" becomes "Falabeet".
- **CODE TYPE 7:** Swap the last letter of each word with the first letter of the next word.

★ THE ★ CHALLENGE!

USING DOOGAN'S *DANGER JOURNAL,* IDENTIFY *WHICH CODES HAVE BEEN USED* TO SCRAMBLE THE MYSTERY MESSAGE. WHAT DOES IT SAY?

ADVENTURE PROGRESS *35%*

FUEL FRENZY

PUZZLE No.14

DOOGAN IS ABOUT TO TELL ABBEY OF THE MESSAGE HE INTERCEPTED, WHEN SHE CRIES OUT...

I CAN SEE THE EXHAUST TRAILS OF THE OTHER PLANES UP AHEAD, DOOGAN. WE'RE GAINING ON THEM!

MOMENTS LATER, CHECKPOINT WETFOOT COMES LOOMING OVER THE HORIZON!

?!

DESPITE A SAFE LANDING, DOOGAN HAS A LONG WAY TO GO TO REGAIN THE LEAD!

LEADER BOARD
By order of A.R. INDUSTRIES Limited

1ST – JAKOBS
2ND – TOOLA
3RD – GOUDA
4TH – MARLIN
5TH – KARMANN
6TH – DOOGAN

* As recorded at Checkpoint Wetfoot.

HUH ... ALL THE PLANES ARE OUT OF FUEL. THERE MUST BE A SECRET STASH AROUND HERE SOMEWHERE FOR US TO FIND!

CHECKPOINT WETFOOT

KEY STAIRS WALL DOOR

START HERE

YOU CAN WALK PAST STAIRS AND DOORS, AND YOU CAN JUMP ACROSS THE TOP OF A STAIRWELL, BUT YOU CANNOT WALK THROUGH WALLS!

★ THE CHALLENGE! ★

DOOGAN HAS A BLUEPRINT FOR CHECKPOINT WETFOOT, AND DISCOVERS THAT CERTAIN DOORS LINK TO EACH OTHER, AS INDICATED BY THE SYMBOLS ON THEM. FOR EXAMPLE, IF YOU GO THROUGH DOOR 22, YOU COME OUT AT DOOR 4. LOOKING AT THE MAP, CAN YOU FIGURE OUT THE ORDER OF THE DOOR NUMBERS DOOGAN MUST ENTER AND EXIT TO ARRIVE AT THE FUEL TANKS?

ADVENTURE PROGRESS 38%

TANGLED TROUBLE

WITH THE STASH OF *EMERGENCY FUEL* LOCATED, VON DOOGAN AND THE OTHER FLIERS FILL THE LARGE ON-DECK *FUEL PUMP*...

THAT'S THE *LOT!* ABBEY SHOULD BE DONE CONNECTING THE HOSES BY NOW...

JUST AS THE PUMP'S MOTOR ROARS INTO LIFE, DOOGAN NOTICES THE *PUMP TANK* IS FAR FROM FULL...

EMPTY — FULL

DOOGAN LOOKS AT THE *DESTINATION DECODER* AND SEES HOW MUCH FUEL IS NEEDED BY EACH PLANE FOR THE NEXT LEG OF THE JOURNEY!

625 MILES TO CHECKPOINT 3. AVERAGE TOP SPEED OF PLANES: 250 MILES PER HOUR. FUEL CONSUMPTION AT TOP SPEED, PER PLANE: 200 GALLONS PER HOUR.

OUR HERO COUNTS UP *HOW MANY* BARRELS HAVE BEEN EMPTIED INTO THE PUMP...

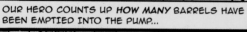

...AND FINALLY CHECKS HIS *CONVERSION CHART*...

A BARREL HOLDS 250 LITRES

LITRES TO GALLONS CONVERSION

1 GALLON = (APPROX.) 5 LITRES

RUSHING TO THE FUEL HOSES, EACH PILOT GRABS ONE AND RUNS TO THEIR PLANE, THE LONG, TANGLED PIPES UNRAVELLING BEHIND THEM AS THEY GO. HOWEVER, SOME OF THE HOSES ARE *MORE TANGLED* THAN OTHERS...

DOOGAN!

GOUDA!

KARMANN!

TOOLA!

MARLIN!

JAKOBS!

★ THE CHALLENGE! ★

ANSWER THE FOLLOWING QUESTIONS!
1: *HOW MANY* BARRELS OF OIL WERE POURED INTO THE PUMP?
2: HOW MANY *LITRES* OF OIL DOES THAT ADD UP TO?
3: HOW MANY *GALLONS* OF OIL IS THAT?
4: HOW MANY *PLANES* WILL THAT FUEL FOR THE *NEXT LEG* OF THE JOURNEY?
5: LOOK CLOSELY AT THE HOSES. WHEN STRETCHED OUT, SOME WILL *KNOT*, SOME WILL *NOT*. WHO WILL BE LEFT *WITHOUT* FUEL?

ADVENTURE PROGRESS 40%

THE CODED BOX

ANOTHER FLIER IS OUT OF THE GREAT AIR RACE! IT'S BECOMING *INCREASINGLY OBVIOUS* TO DOOGAN THAT *ONE OR MORE* OF THE REMAINING PILOTS ARE WORKING TO *SABOTAGE* THEIR COMPETITORS' CHANCES! HOWEVER, THE DOOG'S MIND IS CURENTLY ON OTHER MATTERS...

ACCORDING TO THE *DESTINATION DECODER,* THIS LETTER GRID SHOULD HOLD THE *ROUTE* TO THE NEXT CHECKPOINT!

PORT — A
BONE PASS
PORT — B
C — CRAB ROCK
PORT — D
DEAD MAN'S COVE
CRAB COVE

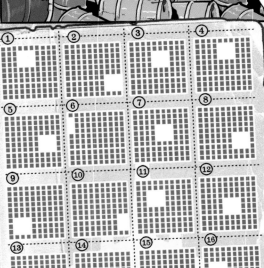

CHECKPOINT JIMJAM
TOP SECRET DESTINATION GRID!

```
X O T R W V N K A U
T C S B U E R E P Q
D P P S D L T P O T
N T S P W T L S H N
C G U O B M R C T S
L O M O D V T N U L
E K O H A E R I J F
I A A A I H I S T E
R H O G A A N F A N
A E D C N B O O P A
```

ROUTE CODE TO JIMJAM!
6,15,2,16,8,11. 1,20,13,18,4.
6,2,7,14,10,19. 1,15,3,12,5,9,13,17.

MESSAGE SQUARE
UP

When the message square is placed over the destination grid in any of the 20 positions above it will reveal a word made up of the letters *outside each of it's corners.* (see diagram)

Read the letters in this order: ■ ● ▲ ★

EXAMPLE 1: SQUARE FULLY ON GRID
WORD: "WITH"

EXAMPLE 2: PARTIALLY ON GRID
WORD: "GO"

★ THE CHALLENGE! ★

1: WHAT DOES THE ROUTE CODE TO JIMJAM *SAY?*
2: AT WHICH *LOCATION* ON THE MAP (A, B, C OR D) IS CHECKPOINT JIMJAM?

ADVENTURE PROGRESS *43*%

THE REMAINING PLANES TAKE OFF FROM CHECKPOINT WETFOOT, AND SOON NIGHT FALLS ON THIS THIRD LEG OF THE AIR RACE.

RUSHING TO THE **STORAGE BAY**, DOOGAN DESPERATELY HUNTS FOR SOMETHING TO AID THEM IN THEIR PREDICAMENT!

WHOEVER'S BEHIND THESE "ACCIDENTS" IS CERTAINLY A SLIPPERY CUSTOMER. I'M GOING TO NEED TO WATCH MY STEP FROM HERE ON...

SUDDENLY, ABBEY'S CRY SHAKES DOOGAN'S PONDERING...

FOG!

THE CHALLENGE!

USING THE **DIAGRAM** BELOW, HELP DOOGAN CHOOSE WISELY FROM THE ITEMS ABOVE. BY SELECTING **CERTAIN** ITEMS, THERE IS **ONE ESCAPE OPTION** DOOGAN CAN TAKE THAT DOES **NOT** INVOLVE CRASHING THE PLANE — WHICH IS IT?

WITHIN MINUTES...

THIS IS *BAD*, ABBEY. I CAN'T SEE THE AIRFIELD! EVEN IN THIS FOG WE SHOULD BE ABLE TO MAKE OUT THE LIGHTS!

THINK FAST, DOOGAN, I'M GETTING STATIC ON THE RADIO, AND WE'RE RUNNING ON GAS FUMES!

THE BIG JUMP

IMPOSSIBILITY LEVEL:

THE THUNDERBOLT'S HEAVY PASSENGER DOOR HAS BEEN FLUNG OPEN, IN EVERY DIRECTION LIES FOG, DARKNESS, AND *DANGER!*

WHO THEN, WOULD BE BOLD ENOUGH TO STEP INTO THIS *TERRIBLE VOID?*

WHY, *VON DOOGAN,* OF COURSE!

THE RULES!

A) Cut out the six playing pieces (five FOG CLOUDS, and DOOGAN). Alternatively, use coins, marking one as the Doog!

B) Place DOOGAN on the spot marked with a "D" and the five FOG CLOUDS on the RED ARROWS, with the arrow on each fog cloud pointing in the SAME DIRECTION as the arrow they are placed on.

C) Each turn FIRST move *ALL FIVE* FOG CLOUD pieces *ONE SPACE*, then move the DOOGAN piece *ONE SPACE*, obeying the rules below:

1) The *FOG CLOUDS* move left and right across the sky IN THE DIRECTION THEIR ARROW IS POINTING. When they land on a square IN FRONT of a STATIC (WHITE) cloud, or get to the EDGE of the board, turn the cloud around so the arrow is pointing in the OPPOSITE direction, and NEXT TURN move the cloud back in that direction.

2) YOU choose the path DOOGAN takes, BUT he can ONLY move *STRAIGHT DOWN, LEFT* or *RIGHT.* IMPORTANT! Doogan CAN move left or right into a square he has occupied before.

A B C D E F G

★ THE CHALLENGE! ★

WHICH IS THE *FIRST* GROUND SQUARE DOOGAN CAN REACH *WITHOUT* MOVING INTO A SPACE OCCUPIED BY A STATIC CLOUD OR A FOG CLOUD PIECE, OR HAVING A FOG CLOUD PIECE MOVING INTO A SQUARE OCCUPIED BY HIM?!

TO *COMPLETE* THIS CHALLENGE YOU'LL NEED TO GRAB THE *PLAYING PIECES* FROM...

DOOGAN'S DANGER KIT

GO TO PAGE → **47**

ADVENTURE PROGRESS *48%*

PUZZLE No. 19 — CROSSED WIRES

 IMPOSSIBILITY LEVEL:

DOOGAN *LITERALLY* HITS THE GROUND RUNNING, SPRINTING TOWARDS THE *CHECKPOINT JIMJAM AIR FIELD...!*

OUT OF SIGHT IN THE *ICY DARKNESS* ABOVE HIM CIRCLE THE OTHER AIR RACERS, THEIR *FUEL RESERVES* DEPLETING RAPIDLY! THE DOOG *MUST* REMEDY THE AIRFIELD'S BLACKOUT!

BEFORE HE RUNS OUT ONTO THE RUNWAY TO LIGHT HIS FLARES, DOOGAN TAKES A QUICK LOOK INSIDE THE DESERTED AIR TOWER. STUDYING THE CONTROL DESK, AND HIS *DANGER JOURNAL,* DOOGAN REALISES THAT THE POWER CUT MAY *NOT* BE AS PERMANENT AS IT SEEMS!

WIRING DIAGRAMS

FOR HIGH-POWER PERFORMANCE IN STANDARD ELECTRICAL SET-UPS.

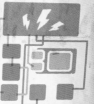

ANY CABLE CAN BE PLUGGED IN TO *ANY* SOCKET, OR *REMOVED COMPLETELY* TO CREATE ONE OF THE CIRCUITS ON THESE PAGES.

★ THE CHALLENGE! ★

IF DOOGAN'S HUNCH IS *RIGHT,* WHAT IS THE *EASIEST* WAY TO GET THE RUNWAY LIGHTS WORKING AGAIN?

ADVENTURE PROGRESS *51%*

SPLASH DOWN

AGAINST ALL THE ODDS OUR PAL **VON DOOGAN** HAS MANAGED TO GET THE CHECKPOINT JIMJAM RUNWAY LIGHTS *WORKING!*

TO HIS *SHOCK*, HOWEVER...! BY THE *FIERY WINGS* OF A FLAMING *PHOENIX!* ABBEY'S ALREADY LANDED! AND SO HAVE ALL BUT ONE OF THE OTHER FLYERS!

WHAT *ON EARTH* IS GOING ON?!

DOOGAN IS JUST ABOUT TO HEAD DOWN TO THE AIRFIELD TO *INVESTIGATE* WHEN...

CZZZZZZRT ... REPEAT ... DO YOU READ ME .... BZZZZZZT .... ANYONE OUT THERE? ... SOS ... *SOS* ... CRZZZKT ... AM IN NEED OF *IMMEDIATE* ASSISTANCE, OVER ... BZZZZT!

THE RADIO! THAT'S *TOOLA'S* VOICE! SHE'S IN *TROUBLE!*

JIMJAM TOWER CALLING *CLOUD HOPPER!* WHAT IS YOUR SITUATION? OVER!

BZZZZZZT ... AM OUT OF *FUEL*, TOWER, 5,000 FEET UP ... GOT PUSHED OFF COURSE BY THE FOG ... BZZT ... KZZZZZZT ... GOING TO HAVE TO HEAD FOR THE COAST AND *BAIL OUT* OVER WATER ... OVER!

UNDERSTOOD, TOOLA. *WHAT ARE YOUR COORDINATES?* OVER!

KZZZT ... *LOSING YOUR SIGNAL*, TOWER ... ZZZZT!

HELLO...? *HELLO?* CLOUD HOPPER, WHAT ARE YOUR COORDINATES? REPEAT – WHAT ARE YOUR COORDINATES? OVER!

BZZZZZZT ... UNSURE OF *POSITION* ... AM FLYING *WEST* OVER LAND TOWARDS WATER ... TWIN-PEAKED MOUNTAIN DIRECTLY TO *NORTH* ... CRZZZZZT ... CAN SEE A SANDY BAY *BELOW* ME, AM GOING TO BAIL OUT AS SOON AS I PASS IT ... TEMP DIAL'S PRETTY LOW, THE WATER WILL BE FREEZING! KRZZZZT ... WISH ME LUCK!

TOOLA WON'T SURVIVE LONG IN THE *ICY SEAS* OFF JIMJAM BAY! DOOGAN KNOWS HE MUST SEND A LIFEBOAT OUT TO HER *FAST*...!

GUARANTEED SURVIVAL TIMES BASED ON WATER TEMPERATURE:
0°C ....7 minutes
5°C .... 10 minutes
10°C.......... 20 minutes

JIM JAM BAY

DURATION OF A PARCHUTE JUMP
FREEFALL:
First 1,000ft = 10 seconds
Each subsequent 1,000ft = 5 seconds
ONCE PARACHUTE IS OPENED:
15 ft per second.

Parachute should be open at 3,000ft.

WINDSPEED VERY LOW, SO FREEFALL/PARACHUTE WILL DROP VERTICALLY WITHOUT BEING BLOWN AROUND.

★ THE ★ CHALLENGE!

1: TO *WHICH CO-ORDINATES (X,Y)* SHOULD DOOGAN SEND A *LIFEBOAT?*
2: *HOW LONG* DO THEY HAVE TO SAVE TOOLA FROM THE MOMENT SHE JUMPS? (MINUTES, SECONDS)

ADVENTURE PROGRESS 54%

PICK-A-TRUCK

IMPOSSIBILITY LEVEL:

TOOLA WAS SAVED, BUT HER PLANE, THE *CLOUD HOPPER*, WAS LOST, AND SHE'S OUT OF THE RACE! THE MYSTERY OF THE THUNDERBOLT LANDING IN THE *BLACKOUT* IS EXPLAINED BY ABBEY, WHO TELLS DOOGAN THAT THE LIGHTS CAME BACK ON *MOMENTARILY* JUST AFTER HE HAD JUMPED.

MORNING COMES, AND WITH IT THE CURIOUS INSTRUCTIONS FOR THE NEXT STAGE OF THE RACE!

WELL! IT LOOKS LIKE THIS PART OF THE JOURNEY WILL BE TRAVELLED BY *ROAD!*

AND WITH ONE OF YOU LOT THROWING A *SPANNER* IN THE WORKS AT EVERY TURN, I'VE A FEELING THERE'LL BE EVEN *MORE* TROUBLE THAN WHEN WE WERE AIRBORNE!

MARLIN! KARMANN! GOUDA!

DOOGAN AND THE OTHER RACERS MUST PARTIALLY DISMANTLE THEIR PLANES AND LOAD THEM ONTO *TRANSPORT TRAILERS*. THERE ARE SEVERAL HEAVY-DUTY *TRUCK CABS* DOOGAN COULD HIRE TO PULL THE LOAD, BUT HE MUST CHOOSE *WISELY!*

1. Green-O

Hire Cost: £20
Total Fuel Cost: £10
Maximum Pull Weight: 4 Tons
Top speed with full load: 80mph

2. Big Red

Hire Cost: £45
Total Fuel Cost: £20
Maximum Pull Weight: 8 Tons
Top speed with full load: 50mph

DOOGAN'S DOUGH
FOR EMERGENCIES ONLY!
Contents:
£120

THUNDERBOLT
Total Weight: 17 tons

3. Flattie

Hire Cost: £40
Total Fuel Cost: £15
Maximum Pull Weight: 7 Tons
Top speed with full load: 60mph

4. The Long Boy

Hire Cost: £40
Total Fuel Cost: £15
Maximum Pull Weight: 9 Tons
Top speed with full load: 55mph

5. White 'Un

Hire Cost: £25
Total Fuel Cost: £15
Maximum Pull Weight: 3 Tons
Top speed with full load: 60mph

6. Hi-Top

Hire Cost: £50
Total Fuel Cost: £20
Maximum Pull Weight: 9 Tons
Top speed with full load: 45mph

7. Long Back

Hire Cost: £40
Total Fuel Cost: £25
Maximum Pull Weight: 9 Tons
Top speed with full load: 45mph

★ **THE CHALLENGE!** ★

WHICH ARE THE *FASTEST TWO* TRUCKS DOOGAN CAN AFFORD TO HIRE?

ADVENTURE PROGRESS **56%**

A HEAVY LOAD

PUZZLE No. 22

IMPOSSIBILITY LEVEL:

WITH THE THUNDERBOLT DISMANTLED AND CRATED UP, THE CONVOY IS READY TO ROLL! SUDDENLY, ONE OF THE ROAD CREW COMES *RUNNING OVER...*

THERE'S A PROBLEM WITH *THE LONG BOY TRAILER,* MR DOOGAN, WE JUST CAN'T SEEM TO GET EVERYTHING TO FIT!

TO *COMPLETE THIS CHALLENGE* YOU'LL NEED THE SIX CRATES FROM

DOOGAN'S DANGER KIT

Quick! GO TO PAGE ➤ 47

HOW TO LOAD THE CRATES

Cut out (or trace around) the six crates and arrange them so they make a *perfect* rectangle, as indicated by the *red dotted area*. The *dark* sides of the crates *can* be covered, but *all* the *light* sides should be visible.

✓ Only covering *dark side*

✗ Covering part of *light side*

LENGTH OF LOAD

HEIGHT OF LOAD

★ THE ★ CHALLENGE!

WITH ALL THE CRATES IN PLACE, A *MESSAGE* WILL BE REVEALED, RUNNING AROUND THE *OUTSIDE* OF THE CARGO, (STARTING AT THE *TOP LEFT CORNER*). WHAT IS IT?

ADVENTURE PROGRESS 59%

PUZZLE No. 23 A RIFT IN THE DRIFT

IMPOSSIBILITY LEVEL:

WAGONS ROLL! THE CONVOY OF GIANT TRUCKS SETS OFF UP THE STEEP MOUNTAIN ROAD. ITS DESTINATION: CHECKPOINT WHITEOUT...!

BUT BEFORE LONG A BLIZZARD OF IMPENETRABLE SNOW LASHES ACROSS DOOGAN'S PATH...
IT'S NO GOOD! WE'RE GOING TO HAVE TO MAKE CAMP IN THE TRUCK TONIGHT AND WAIT IT OUT!

BUT WHEN MORNING COMES...
DOOGAN! WE'RE STUCK FAST, AND THE SNOW SHOVELS I STRAPPED TO THE TRUCK HAVE DISAPPEARED! WE'LL HAVE TO GIVE UP!

VON DOOGAN, *GIVE UP?* WE KNOW OUR HERO BETTER THAN *THAT*, DON'T WE, CHUMS?! SCRAMBLING ONTO THE ROOF OF THE TRUCK, THE DOOG SKETCHES A *DIAGRAM* OF THE *SNOW DRIFT* AND THE ROAD AHEAD. THEN, OPENING ONE OF THE STORAGE CRATES, HE PULLS OUT THE THUNDERBOLT'S *THREE POWERFUL HEATERS...*

HINT – USE A SCRAP OF PAPER TO ***MEASURE*** THINGS!

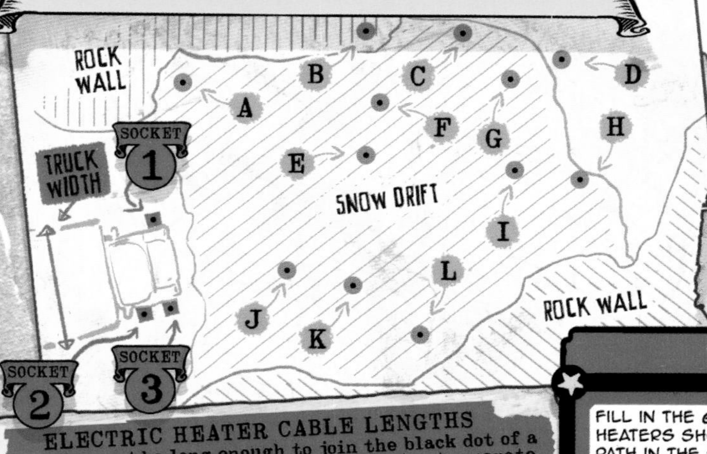
ROCK WALL
A
B
C
D
E
F
G
H
I
J
K
L
SNOW DRIFT
ROCK WALL
TRUCK WIDTH
SOCKET 1
SOCKET 2
SOCKET 3

MAMMOTH BLOWER HEAT RANGE CIRCUMFERENCE
MOUSE BLOWER HEAT RANGE CIRCUMFERENCE

- There are **3** heaters (**2** Mammoth Blowers and **1** Mouse Blower).
- There are **12** possible ***locations*** for the heaters to be placed (labelled A – L).
- Each heater ***must*** plug into one of the truck's power sockets.

ELECTRIC HEATER CABLE LENGTHS

Cable ***must*** be long enough to join the black dot of a ***socket*** to the black dot of a ***location*** to operate.

MAMMOTH BLOWER 1 ⟷

MAMMOTH BLOWER 2 ⟷

THE MOUSE BLOWER ⟷

THE CHALLENGE!

FILL IN THE *GAPS BELOW* TO DESCRIBE *WHERE* THE HEATERS SHOULD BE *PLACED AND PLUGGED IN* TO MELT A PATH IN THE SNOW DRIFT *WIDE ENOUGH* FOR THE TRUCK TO PASS THROUGH.

MAMMOTH BLOWER 1 – LOCATION: ____ SOCKET: ____

MAMMOTH BLOWER 2 – LOCATION: ____ SOCKET: ____

MOUSE BLOWER – LOCATION: ____ SOCKET: ____

ADVENTURE PROGRESS 62%

PUZZLE No. 24
BOULDER OF DOOM

IMPOSSIBILITY LEVEL:

DOOGAN HAS CAUGHT UP WITH THE OTHER RACERS! THEY SCALE THE *FINAL MILES* OF THE TREACHEROUS MOUNTAIN ROAD, UNAWARE THAT A HUGE BALL OF *ROCKY TERROR* IS HURTLING TOWARDS THEM!

A) Cut out the FIVE playing pieces. These represent the four racers, and the boulder. Alternatively, use coins.

B) Place each piece on their *starting space*.

TO *COMPLETE THIS CHALLENGE* YOU'LL NEED THE *PLAYING PIECES* FROM...
DOOGAN'S DANGER KIT
GO TO PAGE ➤ **47**

C) Each turn FIRST move *ALL FOUR RACER* pieces, then move the BOULDER piece, obeying the rules below:

1) The racers move at *different* speeds *along the path*:
DOOGAN – 3 spaces.
GOUDA – 2 spaces.
KARMANN – 4 spaces.
MARLIN – 1 space.
They *CAN* occupy the same space as each other.

2) The BOULDER moves one space each turn, following the red path.

3) If a racer *LANDS ON*, or *MOVES THROUGH* a square containing the boulder, or the boulder *LANDS ON THEM*, they *COLLIDE!*

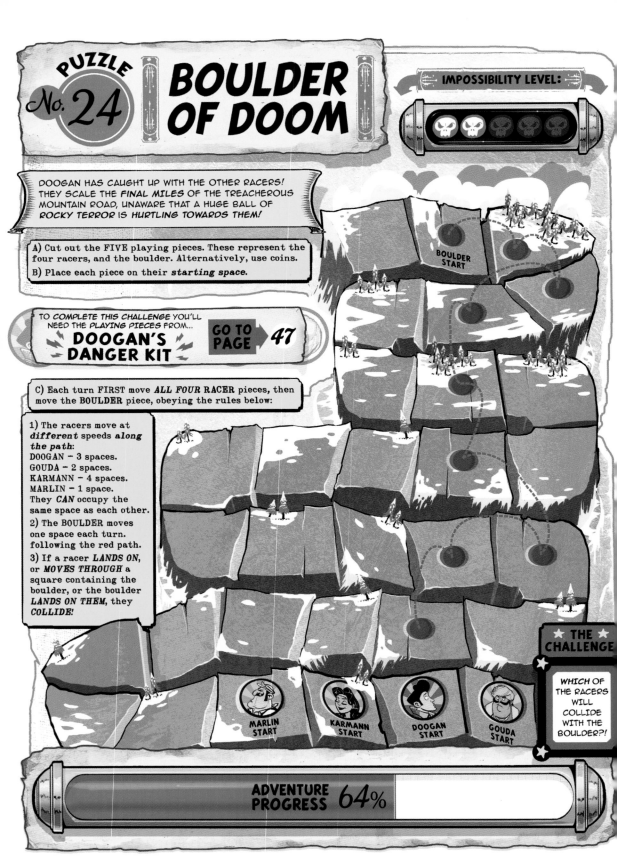

BOULDER START

MARLIN START

KARMANN START

DOOGAN START

GOUDA START

★ THE ★ CHALLENGE

WHICH OF THE RACERS WILL COLLIDE WITH THE BOULDER?!

ADVENTURE PROGRESS *64%*

THE MISSING CRATE MYSTERY

ARRIVING AT CHECKPOINT WHITEOUT, DOOGAN AND THE REMAINING TWO FLYING TEAMS SET ABOUT REBUILDING THE PLANES...

OH, THE THUNDERBOLT'S NEARLY BACK TOGETHER, CHIEF. SHE'S JUST MISSING TWO CRATES OF PARTS...

WAIT... **WHAT?!**

TAM TAM TAM

IT'S LOOKING GOOD, GUYS! HOW LONG UNTIL SHE'S READY TO FLY?

PIM POM PAM

DOOGAN PULLS FROM HIS POCKET VARIOUS NOTES HE HAD MADE DURING THE PACKING OF THE THREE PLANES, AND TRIES TO FIGURE OUT JUST WHERE THE TWO MISSING *THUNDERBOLT CRATES* HAVE GONE...

Packing Totals:

Total crates per plane after dismantling:

Firefly: 16 Crates

Thunderbolt: 18 Crates

Sky King: 15 crates

BREAK-DOWN OF THUNDERBOLT

CRATES A – D

CRATES L – P

CRATES E – K

CRATES Q – R

PACKING SLIP

Crates A – D for SK delivered to P. Mooran

Crates A – D for T delivered to B. Pooche

Crates A – D for F delivered to W. Greene

TRUCK LOAD CAPACITY		TRUCK LOAD CAPACITY	
FLATTIE	8 CRATES	BIG RED	7 CRATES
HI-TOP	7 CRATES	LONG BACK	9 CRATES

TRUCK LOAD CAPACITY
THE LONG BOY.....9 CRATES
WHITE 'UN.............9 CRATES

PLANE: THUNDERBOLT
TRUCKS HIRED FOR TRANSPORT:
"BIG RED" AND "THE LONG BOY"

PLANE: FIREFLY
TRUCKS HIRED FOR TRANSPORT:
"WHITE 'UN" AND "LONG BACK"

PLANE: SKY KING
TRUCKS HIRED FOR TRANSPORT:
"FLATTIE" AND "HI-TOP"

PACKING SLIP

Crates E – M for SK delivered to P. Moor...

Crates E – P for T delivered to B. Pooch...

Crates E – P for F delivered to W. Green...

Hauling Truck Team Leaders:
Wally Greene – FIREFLY
Barney Pooche – THUNDERBOLT
Pongo Mooran – SKY KING

Crates for each of the 3 planes are labelled alphabetically.

PACKING

Crates N – P f... delivered to P. M...

Crates Q – R delivered to...

★ THE CHALLENGE!

STUDY THE INFORMATION ABOVE, AND ANSWER THESE QUESTIONS:
1) WHICH PLANE HAS THE TWO MISSING *THUNDERBOLT CRATES*?
2) WHICH CRATES ARE THEY (A, B, C ETC)?

ADVENTURE PROGRESS 67%

THE FINAL DESTINATION

IMPOSSIBILITY LEVEL:

ALL THREE PLANES ARE FINALLY BACK TOGETHER, HOWEVER, THE *LOCATION* OF THE FINAL DESTINATION IS AS YET *UNKNOWN*...

LEADER BOARD
By order of
A.R. INDUSTRIES
Limited

1ST – KARMANN
2ND – DOOGAN
3RD – MARLIN
~~4TH – GOUDA~~
~~5TH – TOBIN~~
~~6TH – JAKOBS~~
~~7TH – WELDON~~
~~8TH – WINGS~~

★ As recorded at Checkpoint Whiteout.

WELL, *GOOD LUCK*, BOTH OF YOU, AND MAY THE *BEST PILOT WIN*. SHAKE?

SHAKE HANDS?! NOT LIKELY! I'VE GOT YOU PEGGED AS THE *SABOTEUR*, DOOGAN!

AND HOW DO WE KNOW THAT *YOU* AREN'T THE GUILTY PARTY, MARLIN?!

ME?! WHAT NONSENSE, KARMANN! ANYWAY, WE'VE NO TIME TO WORRY ABOUT ALL THAT – HERE COME OUR *TOP SECRET* DESTINATION DROPS!

DOOGAN TEARS OPEN THE CURIOUS BUNDLE AND STARES *BEWILDERED* AT THE CONTENTS...

HMMM ... IT LOOKS LIKE THIS MIGHT BE THE *TOUGHEST* PUZZLE YET!

DEAR *Von Doogan*,
TO DISCOVER THE **FINAL DESTINATION**, SOLVE THE 4 PUZZLE SQUARES IN ORDER.

1: EACH PUZZLE SQUARE HAS A GRID OF *BROWN BLOCKS* INSIDE A WOODEN FRAME, AND SEVERAL *GREEN BLOCKS* OUTSIDE IT.

2: TO SOLVE EACH PUZZLE YOU MUST REMOVE **ALL** THE BLOCKS WITH "X"S FROM THE CENTRAL GRID BY PUSHING *EACH* OF THE GREEN BLOCKS ONCE, IN A SPECIFIC ORDER.

3: NOTE DOWN THE *CORRECT ORDER* IN WHICH YOU PUSH THE GREEN BLOCKS.

THIS EXAMPLE: P, W

4: WRITE DOWN **ALL** THE LETTERS FOR ALL THE PUZZLES IN THE ORDER YOU PUSHED THEM.

★ **THE CHALLENGE!** ★

READ THE CODE BELOW *BACKWARDS* – WHAT DOES IT SAY?

WRITE THE LETTERS ON A SCRAP OF PAPER LIKE THIS!

ADVENTURE PROGRESS *70%*

FLAG FLUMMOX

IMPOSSIBILITY LEVEL:

WITH ABBEY FINALISING THE GROUND CHECKS, *DOOGAN* WARMS UP THE ENGINES FOR THE PERILOUS CHECKPOINT WHITEOUT *TAKE-OFF...*

WELL, *THUNDERBOLT* OLD GIRL, THIS IS IT. EVERYTHING DEPENDS ON *YOU* NOW, I JUST HOPE YOU CAN HOLD TOGETHER LONG ENOUGH TO GET US OVER THAT *FINISH LINE!*

SUDDENLY, OUR HERO NOTICES SOMETHING *VERY STRANGE...*

THAT'S FUNNY, FOR A MOMENT I THOUGHT I SAW ... NO, *WAIT! THERE IT IS AGAIN!* SOMEONE'S OUT THERE – AND THEY'RE SENDING A MESSAGE!

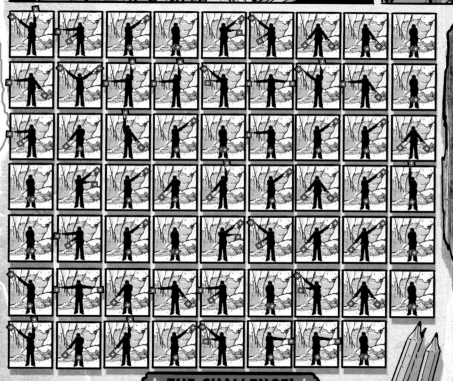

SEMAPHORE

A		H	
B		I	
C		J	
D		K	
E		L	
F		M	
G		N	

O		V	
P		W	
Q		X	
R		Y	
S		Z	
T		BREAK	
U			

★ THE CHALLENGE! ★

DOOGAN DECODES THE MESSAGE AND REALISES THAT IT ISN'T *FOR* HIM, BUT THAT IT COULD BE *ABOUT* HIM! RUSHING TO CHECK THE THUNDERBOLT HE FINDS THAT EVERYTHING IS OKAY, MEANING THAT EITHER *MARLIN* OR *KARMANN* ARE IN *DANGER!*

 MARLIN!

WHO IS IN DANGER? – OR –

 KARMANN!

ADVENTURE PROGRESS *72%*

DEAD WEIGHT

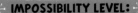

HAVING SAVED *MARLIN* FROM CERTAIN DEATH, DOOGAN *FINALLY* KNOWS THE IDENTITY OF THE GREAT AIR RACE SABOTEUR...!

SO, KARMANN, IT WAS *YOU* ALL ALONG! LOOKS LIKE YOU'VE BEEN DEALING OUT *COLD BLOODED VILLAINY* FROM THE VERY START...

... BUT *THE DOOG'S* ON YOUR TRAIL NOW, AND HE'S BRINGING HIS FRIEND, MR *RETRIBUTION!*

THE MIGHTY *THUNDERBOLT* CLAWS HER WAY INTO THE AIR ONE FINAL TIME, AND OUR HERO IS AWAY!

LEADER BOARD
By order of
A.R. INDUSTRIES
Limited

1ST – KARMANN
2ND – DOOGAN
~~3RD – MARLIN~~
~~4TH – SOUZA~~
~~5TH – TOOL~~
~~6TH – JACOB~~
~~7TH – WRIGHT~~
~~8TH – KLAUS~~

★ As recorded at Checkpoint Whiteout.

HOWEVER, THE *VITAL MINUTES* LOST IN ALERTING MARLIN TO THE DANGER HE FACED HAVE COST DOOGAN DEARLY...

YOU TAKE THE CONTROLS, ABBEY, AND *GUN THE ENGINES FOR ALL THEY'RE WORTH!* I'M GOING TO SEE IF I CAN BUY US SOME MORE *SPEED* WITH A LITTLE CARGO PURGE...

IN THE CARGO BAY...

NOW, JUST WHAT CAN WE AFFORD TO *LOSE* FROM THIS LOT?

Liquid Weights
FUEL:
10 GALLONS = 61 LBS
- - - - - -
OIL:
10 GALLONS = 70 LBS
- - - - - -
WATER:
10 GALLONS = 85 LBS

THUNDERBOLT CARGO LIST

TOOL KITS
136 LBS PER BUNDLE

FUEL
100 GALLONS PER CAN

HANG GLIDER KIT
127 LBS IN TOTAL

WATER
10 GALLONS PER TANK

SPARE PARTS
150 LBS PER CRATE

OIL
30 GALLONS PER TANK

THUNDERBOLT **CONSUMTION LEVELS** DURING FLIGHT.

200 GALLONS OF FUEL
20 GALLONS OF OIL
20 GALLONS OF WATER
FOR EVERY 250 MILES TRAVELLED

DISTANCE TO CHECKPOINT HOWHI:	**375 MILES**

THE CHALLENGE!

DOOGAN JETTISONS EVERYTHING BUT THE FUEL, OIL AND WATER NEEDED TO GET TO CHECKPOINT HOWHI.
1. *HOW MUCH LIGHTER* IS THE PLANE NOW?
2. WHAT IS HER *NEW TOP SPEED?*

THE THUNDERBOLT
CURRENT WEIGHT (INC. CARGO)
35,000 LBS

CURRENT TOP SPEED
250MPH

GAINS 1 MPH IN SPEED FOR EVERY 140 LBS IN WEIGHT LOST.

ADVENTURE PROGRESS *75%*

PUZZLE No. 29 — THE BIG GIVEAWAY

IMPOSSIBILITY LEVEL:

EXHAUSTED FROM JETTISONING THE CARGO, DOOGAN **SLUMPS DOWN** AGAINST THE WALL OF THE STORAGE BAY. AS HE DOES SO, OUR HERO ACCIDENTALLY DISLODGES A **BATTERED BOX**, WHICH HAD BEEN HIDDEN IN THE HOLD.

?!?

OPENING THE LID, DOOGAN IS STRUCK BY A TERRIBLE REALISATION...!

THE BOX CONTAINS SEVERAL ITEMS (IN THE **RED CIRCLES**) WHICH SEEM RELATED TO RECENT "**INCIDENTS**"...!

WHAT'S IN THE BOX...

"OUR HERO REALISED HIS **ALARM CLOCK** HAD BEEN TURNED **OFF** AND HE'D BEEN BARRICADED INTO HIS ROOM!"

QUICK! THE PLANE!

OH! DOOGAN ... THERE YOU ARE. I WAS JUST OUT BUYING US BREAKFAST WHEN I SAW THE **SMOKE**...

SAND

EXTRA STRONG WOOD GLUE

"FORTUNATELY, ABBEY HAD MANAGED TO TAXI THE **THUNDERBOLT** TO SAFETY."

MESSAGE FROM "K" — WHEN I'M ON THE GROUND I'LL TURN THE LIGHTS OUT — ONCE YOU'VE CONVINCED DOOGAN TO JUMP, I'LL PUT THEM ON BRIEFLY FOR YOU TO LAND.

BACK DOOR GLUED SHUT AND LOCKED

"THE DOOG STUMBLES ACROSS A STRANGE BROADCAST, ITS MESSAGE ENCRYPTED IN A MIXTURE OF CODES..."

MESSAGE FROM "K" - TRAP DOOGAN IN THE CHALET AND SET FIRE TO SECRET WING. IN THE ENSUING CHAOS, STEAL THUNDERBOLT.

"**AGAINST ALL THE ODDS**, DOOGAN MANAGED TO PARACHUTE DOWN TO CHECKPOINT **JIMJAM** !"

"TO HIS **SHOCK** HOWEVER...!"

BY THE **FIERY WINGS** OF A FLAMING **PHOENIX**! ABBEY'S ALREADY LANDED! AND SO HAVE ALL BUT ONE OF THE OTHER FLYERS!

I'M TOO BUSY TRYING TO FIND THE **IGNITION KEYS**. THERE ARE **FOUR** OF THEM AROUND HERE SOMEPLACE...

NO. 5

MESSAGE FROM "K" — NEED TO BE MORE CAREFUL. FROM NOW ON WILL USE COMBINATION OF CODES 1 AND 6 TO COMMUNICATE WHEN YOU'RE IN THUNDERBOLT.

"NEXT MORNING ABBEY EXCLAIMS..."

DOOGAN! WE'RE **STUCK FAST**, AND THE SNOW SHOVELS I STRAPPED TO THE TRUCK HAVE **DISAPPEARED!** WE'LL HAVE TO GIVE UP!

SHOVEL STRAP

KNOT-TYING HANDBOOK

"ABOARD THE FLOATING BEHEMOTH **CHECKPOINT WETFOOT**, AND WITH THE STASH OF **EMERGENCY FUEL** LOCATED, VON DOOGAN AND THE OTHER FLIERS FILLED THE LARGE ON-DECK **FUEL PUMP**..."

THAT'S THE LOT! ABBEY SHOULD BE DONE CONNECTING THE HOSES BY NOW...

"HOWEVER, SOME OF THE HOSES WERE MORE TANGLED THAN OTHERS..."

★ THE CHALLENGE! ★

COMPLETE THE SENTENCE BELOW:
"DOOGAN HAS REALISED THAT FROM THE VERY BEGINNING, THE **SABOTAGE** OF THE OTHER RACERS, AND THE ATTEMPTS TO FORCE **HIM** OUT OF THE RACE, HAVE BEEN CARRIED OUT BY KARMANN AND _____ !"

ADVENTURE PROGRESS 78%

COCKPIT LOCKOUT

DOOGAN **BOLTS** OUT OF THE CARGO BAY, FILLED WITH WITH **DREAD** AT THE IMPLICATIONS OF HIS DISCOVERY, AND THE THOUGHT THAT...

...ABBEY'S FLYING THE THUNDERBOLT **RIGHT NOW!** I'VE GOT TO GET TO HER BEFORE SHE HAS A CHANCE TO START ANY MORE **DIABOLICAL MACHINATIONS!**

AS DOOGAN SPRINTS THE LENGTH OF THE MIGHTY PLANE, HE GLANCES OUT OF ONE OF THE SIDE WINDOWS...

WAIT, WHAT'S THAT...?! **HOLY SMOKES!** IT'S ABBEY, AND SHE'S **PARACHUTING AWAY!**

AT THAT MOMENT THE THUNDERBOLT LURCHES ERRATICALLY AND STARTS TO **NOSEDIVE**...

NO ONE AT THE CONTROLS AND ABBEY'S TAKEN OUR LAST PARACHUTE! THIS IS GETTING **WORSE** BY THE MINUTE!

THE DOOG, BATTERED AND **DISORIENTED** FROM FIGHTING AGAINST THE PITCH AND ROLL OF THE STRICKEN PLANE, FINALLY MAKES IT TO THE COCKPIT DOOR...!

WHAT'S THIS? **LOCKED!** AND HOOKED UP TO A **BOMB!** NOW I AM IN A SPOT!

REALISING THAT THE LOCKING DEVICE IS **HOME-MADE**, DOOGAN ROOTS THROUGH ABBEY'S PAPERS AND FINDS A SCHEMATIC OF HOW IT WAS BUILT...

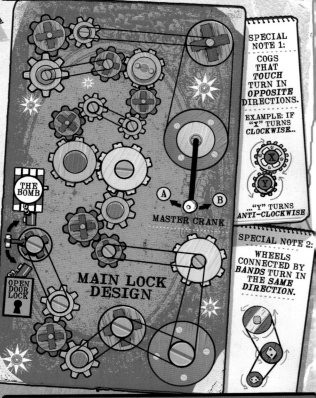

THE BOMB

OPEN DOOR LOCK

MAIN LOCK DESIGN

A B

MASTER CRANK

SPECIAL NOTE 1:

COGS THAT **TOUCH** TURN IN **OPPOSITE** DIRECTIONS.

EXAMPLE: IF "X" TURNS **CLOCKWISE**...

..."Y" TURNS **ANTI-CLOCKWISE**

SPECIAL NOTE 2:

WHEELS CONNECTED BY **BANDS** TURN IN THE **SAME** DIRECTION.

★ THE CHALLENGE! ★

ON THE OUTSIDE OF THE LOCK IS A **MASTER CRANK**. DOOGAN KNOWS THAT IF HE TURNS THE CRANK IN ONE DIRECTION IT WILL **OPEN THE DOOR**, BUT IF HE TURNS IT IN THE OTHER, IT WILL **SET THE BOMB OFF!** USING THE **LOCK DESIGN** SCHEMATIC AS A GUIDE, ALONG WITH THE TWO **SPECIAL NOTES**, CAN YOU FIGURE OUT **WHICH DIRECTION** DOOGAN SHOULD TURN THE MASTER CRANK TO OPEN THE DOOR; TOWARDS "A", OR "B"?

ADVENTURE PROGRESS *80%*

MID-AIR MELTDOWN

BURSTING INTO THE COCKPIT, DOOGAN SEES THAT ABBEY HAS *WRECKED* THE CONTROLS BEYOND ALL REPAIR!

WITH THE MOUNTAIN RANGE DRAWING EVER CLOSER, IT LOOKS LIKE OUR HERO'S FATE IS SEALED.

BUT WAIT, WHAT'S THAT?! JUST AHEAD OF THE THUNDERBOLT, WEAVING ACROSS THE SKY IS...

THE FIREFLY!

SMASHED! WELL, THERE'LL BE *NO SOFT LANDING* FOR YOU OR ME, OLD GIRL!

WITH THE THUNDERBOLT ON A COLLISION COURSE WITH MOUNT HOWHI, DOOGAN TAKES A *DESPERATE* GAMBLE – TO JUMP FROM HIS DOOMED AIRCRAFT AND HITCH A RIDE WITH THE VILLAINOUS KARMANN!

THE THUNDERBOLT

CURRENT FORWARD SPEED:
6,000 METRES A MINUTE
CURRENT DESCENT:
300 METRES A MINUTE

THE FIREFLY

CURRENT FORWARD SPEED:
4,500 METRES A MINUTE
CURRENT DESCENT:
150 METRES A MINUTE

SKY CHART

METRES HIGH

		A 0	B 100	C 200	D 300	E 400	F 500	G 600	H 700	I 800	J 900	K 1,000	L 1,100	M 1,200	N 1,300	O 1,400	P 1,500	Q 1,600	R 1,700	S 1,800	T 1,900	U 2,000

120 13
110 12
100 11
90 10
80 9
70 8
60 7
50 6
40 5
30 4
20 3
10 2
0 1

GRID REFS

METRES TRAVELLED FORWARDS

CHANCE OF SUCCESSFULLY LANDING A FREE JUMP (BASED ON HEIGHT).

0-10 METRES - 100%
11-30 METRES - 50%
31-60 METRES - 20%

★ THE CHALLENGE! ★

ANSWER THE FOLLOWING QUESTIONS:
1: HOW MANY METRES DOES THE *FIREFLY* TRAVEL *FORWARD*, AND HOW MANY METRES DOES IT *DESCEND*, PER SECOND?
2: HOW MANY METRES DOES THE *THUNDERBOLT* TRAVEL *FORWARD*, AND HOW MANY METRES DOES IT *DESCEND*, PER SECOND?
3: BASED ON THEIR POSITIONS ON THE SKY CHART, WHERE (GRID REFS) WILL EACH PLANE BE AFTER 12 SECONDS?
4: IF DOOGAN JUMPED AT THIS POINT, WHAT WOULD BE HIS *CHANCE OF SUCCESS* (AS A PERCENTAGE)?

ADVENTURE PROGRESS 83%

MID-AIR BREAK-IN

IMPOSSIBILITY LEVEL:

TEN ... NINE ... EIGHT ... TENSE SECONDS *COUNT DOWN* AS DOOGAN PREPARES FOR HIS MOST *DARING* FEAT OF BRAVERY YET ... *SEVEN ... SIX ... FIVE* ... HE STEELS HIMSELF, FOCUSES ON THE *FIREFLY* AS IT BOBS AND WEAVES *ERRATICALLY* ON THE WIND BELOW HIM ... *FOUR ... THREE* ... WHISPERS ONE LAST GOODBYE TO THE FAITHFUL *THUNDERBOLT* AND ... *TWO ... ONE ... JUMPS!*

URGH! MADE IT! BUT SNEAKING ON BOARD AND GETTING THE BETTER OF *KARMANN* IS ANOTHER CHALLENGE YET!

WHUM!

I NEED TO MOVE *QUICKLY* – THESE NOTES I TOOK IN THE *DANGER JOURNAL* BACK AT THE *BARLEY AIRFIELD* SHOULD HELP!

DOOGAN KNOWS THAT HE *MUST* GET TO KARMANN BEFORE *SHE* DISCOVERS *HIM!*

IF ANY ALARM IS SET OFF, THE COCKPIT WILL BE SEALED AND THE REST OF THE PLANE FLOODED WITH POISON GAS!

ALARMS ON THE *FIREFLY* ARE ACTIVATED IF THE *HATCH* OR *DOOR* THEY ARE FITTED TO IS *OPENED*

FIREFLY ALARM SYSTEM

KARMANN!

MAXIMUM REACH OF DOOGAN'S ARM

KEY
- ALARM
- DOOR
- ACCESS HATCH, OR WINDOW
- BATTERY ⎓ CONNECTING CABLE

COCKPIT

DOOGAN CAN FIT THROUGH A, C, D AND G, BUT CAN ONLY GET HIS *ARM* THROUGH B, E AND F.

ALARMS CAN *ONLY* BE DISABLED BY REACHING THE *BATTERY* THEY ARE CONNECTED TO AND REMOVING IT.

★ THE CHALLENGE! ★

FILL IN THE GAPS IN THE FOLLOWING SENTENCES: "TO GET TO THE *COCKPIT* WITHOUT SETTING AN *ALARM* OFF, DOOGAN MUST FIRST REACH THROUGH *WINDOW* ▢ AND REMOVE *BATTERY* ▢. HE CAN THEN ENTER THE PLANE THROUGH *HATCH* ▢. NEXT HE MUST REMOVE *BATTERY* ▢ WHICH WILL ALLOW HIM TO GO THROUGH *DOOR* ▢. FINALLY HE MUST CRAWL THROUGH TO *BATTERY* ▢ AND REMOVE IT, SO THAT HE CAN ENTER THE *COCKPIT* THROUGH *DOOR* ▢ AND CATCH KARMANN *UNAWARES*"

ADVENTURE PROGRESS 86%

PUZZLE No. 33

HUNT FOR HOWHI

IMPOSSIBILITY LEVEL:

DOOGAN *BURSTS* INTO THE COCKPIT OF THE FIREFLY AND SAYS...

DOOGAN! I DON'T KNOW HOW YOU GOT *IN HERE*, BUT I KNOW HOW YOU'LL BE *LEAVING*...

KARMANN'S HAND REACHES FOR A PISTOL...

THE GAME'S UP, KARMANN! YOUR DAYS OF AIRBORNE AGITATION ARE AT AN END!

...BUT THE DOOG IS TOO QUICK FOR HER!

NOT SO FAST, MA'AM! I'LL TAKE THIS!

HOWEVER, KARMANN HAS ONE LAST *DECEPTION* TO *DECLARE*...!

HEHEH. YOUR GULLIBILITY HAS BEEN YOUR GREATEST WEAKNESS, DOOGAN! YOU MAY HAVE CONTROL OF THE PLANE, BUT DO YOU *ACTUALLY KNOW WHERE WE ARE?*

OUR PAL GOES AN ICY SHADE OF WHITE!

BY SCOTT, SHE'S RIGHT! IT WAS *ABBEY* WHO PLOTTED OUR FINAL COURSE! IT'S *SURE TO BE FALSE!*

VIEW OUT OF THE FRONT WINDOW OF THE FIREFLY

KARMANN REFUSES TO HELP DOOGAN UNLESS HE HANDS CONTROL OF THE PLANE BACK TO HER. WITH THE FIREFLY'S FUEL *RUNNING OUT*, THE DOOG SEEMS TO HAVE BEEN OUTWITTED! OUR HERO DESPERATELY STUDIES HIS MAP, HOPING THAT BY LOOKING OUT OF THE *COCKPIT WINDOWS*, AND USING THE PLANE'S *COMPASS*, HE MAY BE ABLE TO GET A *BEARING* ON HIS LOCATION!

VIEW OUT OF THE RIGHT WINDOW OF THE FIREFLY

FIREFLY DIRECTION COMPASS

MOUNTAIN RANGE MAP

HOW HI

5 4 3 2 1

Y-AXIS

A B C D E F G

X-AXIS

VIEW OUT OF THE LEFT WINDOW OF THE FIREFLY

★ THE CHALLENGE! ★

ANSWER THESE QUESTIONS:
1. *WHERE* ON THE MAP IS THE FIREFLY (X,Y)
2. IN *WHICH* DIRECTION (NORTH, SOUTH, EAST OR WEST) SHOULD DOOGAN FLY TO REACH MOUNT HOWHI?

ADVENTURE PROGRESS *88%*

37

PUZZLE No. 34

BLAZING MAZE

IMPOSSIBILITY LEVEL:

START

DOOGAN IS JUST ABOUT TO TOUCHDOWN, WHEN HIS FEISTY PRISONER SUDDENLY LUNGES AT HIM...!

THE DOOG'S ATTENTION IS MOMENTARILY DISTRACTED, WITH *DEVASTATING CONSEQUENCES!* THE FIREFLY *CRASHES* DOWN THE MOUNTAIN RUNWAY!

BWAAM!

HISSSSS! I WON'T GO WITHOUT A FIGHT!

KARMANN! NO!

OUR PAL IS THROWN CLEAR AS THE TANKS *EXPLODE!* HE COMES ROUND AMONGST THE WRECKAGE WITH AN *UNCONSCIOUS* KARMANN, AND *FIRE EVERYWHERE!* CAN DOOGAN GET HIMSELF AND KARMANN TO *SAFETY?*

SAFE!

KEY

● FIRE EXTINGUISHER

FIRE WALL

★ THE ★ CHALLENGE!

USING THE *FIRE EXTINGUISHERS* THAT DOOGAN FINDS ALONG THE WAY, HELP OUR HERO CLEAR A SAFE PATH THROUGH THE FIRES, AND ESCAPE THE MAZE OF DEBRIS BEFORE THE WHOLE LOT GOES UP IN *FLAMES!* EACH EXTINGUISHER HAS ENOUGH WATER TO PUT OUT *ONE* WALL OF FIRE, AFTER WHICH IT IS *DISCARDED.* DOOGAN MAY CARRY UP TO *TWO* EXTINGUISHERS AT ONCE. WHEN YOU HAVE FOUND A *SAFE* ROUTE, ANSWER THESE QUESTIONS: 1. *WHICH* OF THE *BLACK NUMBERS* DOES DOOGAN CROSS?
2. *HOW MANY* FIRE EXTINGUISHERS DOES HE USE IN *TOTAL?*

ADVENTURE PROGRESS 91%

DUPLICITOUS DOORS

IMPOSSIBILITY LEVEL:

CARRYING **KARMANN** TO SAFETY, DOOGAN FINDS HIMSELF FACING **THREE** DOORS CARVED INTO THE SIDE OF **MOUNT HOWHI**. SUDDENLY, KARMANN AWAKES IN HIS ARMS...

DOOGAN ... WAIT ... COUGH ... ABBEY ... SHE'S BEEN HERE AHEAD OF YOU ... YOU SAVED MY LIFE, SO I MUST TELL YOU ... THE DOORS ARE ... WHEEEZE ... THE DOORS ARE RIGGED WITH TRAPS! HERE ... THESE CLUES ABBEY SENT ME SHOULD HELP...

DOOGAN STUDIES THE SCRAP OF PAPER KARMANN HANDS HIM...

Top secret message for "K" from "A"

SECRET CLUES FOR DECODING/DISARMING DOORWAY TRAPS

1 IF THERE ARE **MULTIPLE** DOORS, I WILL WRITE A STATEMENT ON EACH ONE. **ONLY ONE OF THE STATEMENTS IS TRUE.** USE THIS FACT TO DISCOVER WHICH DOOR LEADS TO THE EXIT.

2 IF I ATTACH A **CUBE BOMB**, DEACTIVATE IT BY PRESSING THE SIDE INDICATED WITH A **QUESTION MARK** IN THIS VIEW:

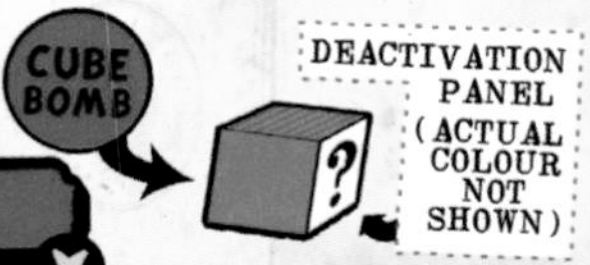

CUBE BOMB

DEACTIVATION PANEL (ACTUAL COLOUR NOT SHOWN)

3 IF I'VE ACTIVATED A **GRID LOCK**, USE THE FOLLOWING INFORMATION TO HELP YOU DECODE IT.

C = 4   F = 6   G = 2

Watch out for trouble, see you at the finish line!

Abbey

★ CHALLENGE ONE! ★

DOOGAN SEES THAT THERE ARE **THREE** DOORS IN TOTAL. EACH DOOR HAS A MESSAGE ON IT. **WHICH** DOOR LEADS TO THE **EXIT?**

A — THIS IS THE EXIT

B — THIS IS NOT THE EXIT

C — DOOR A IS NOT THE EXIT

THE DOOR HAS BEEN FITTED WITH A **SPECIAL LOCK!** ON THE LEFT IS A **GRID** FILLED WITH A COMBINATION OF LETTERS FROM A – I IN THE ALPHABET. EACH OF THE LETTERS HAS A **DIFFERENT** NUMERIC VALUE FROM 1 – 9.

BESIDE EACH ROW, AND BENEATH EACH **COLUMN**, IS THE **SUM** OF THE NUMBERS REPRESENTED BY THE LETTERS IN THAT ROW OR COLUMN.

DOOGAN MUST FIGURE OUT THE **NUMERICAL VALUE** OF **EACH LETTER** ON THE GRID.

ONCE HE HAS DONE THIS HE MUST ENTER THE NUMBERS REPRESENTED BY A, B, C, D, E, F, G, H AND I, **IN THAT ORDER**, INTO THE KEYPAD.

★ CHALLENGE TWO! ★

THERE IS A **CUBE BOMB** ABOVE THE DOOR. DOOGAN LOOKS AT IT FROM **THREE** DIFFERENT ANGLES. USING THESE VIEWS, AND THE **FOURTH VIEW** SHOWN IN ABBEY'S NOTE, WHICH OF THE **COLOURED SIDES** SHOULD DOOGAN PRESS TO **DEACTIVATE** IT?

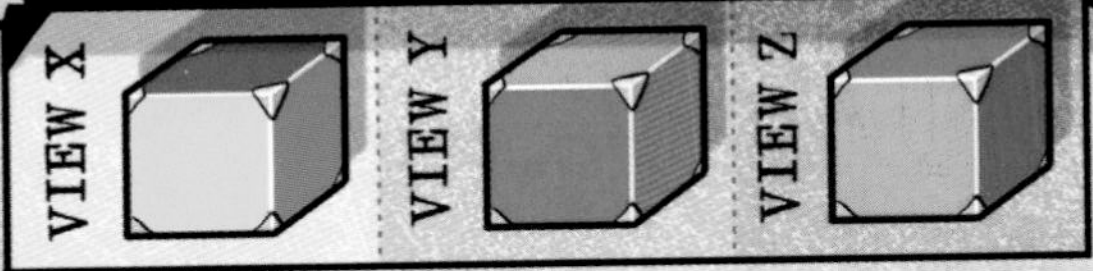

VIEW X

VIEW Y

VIEW Z

E	G	F	I	22
G	H	G	F	18
A	B	I	B	14
H	D	C	C	23
18	18	21	20	

★ CHALLENGE THREE! ★

WHAT IS THE **CORRECT ORDER** IN WHICH DOOGAN MUST ENTER THE **NINE NUMBERS** INTO THE KEYPAD?

ADVENTURE PROGRESS **94%**

PUZZLE No. 36 — THE BIG PARTY

IMPOSSIBILITY LEVEL:

THE RESULTS!

By order of
A.R. INDUSTRIES
Limited

1ST – DOOGAN
2ND – KARMANN
3RD – MARLIN
4TH – GOUDA
5TH – TOOLA
6TH – JAKOBS
7TH – WINGNUT
8TH – KLAUS

★ As recorded at Checkpoint Howhi.

BEHIND THE DOOR, A STAIRCASE RUNS UP THE *INSIDE* OF MOUNT HOWHI! AS DOOGAN ASCENDS THE STAIRS HE DISCOVERS SOME *ODD ITEMS*, SEEMINGLY RECENTLY DISCARDED. SUDDENLY, THE LIGHTS COME ON, AND ... *HUZZAH!* VON DOOGAN HAS *WON THE GREAT AIR RACE!* STILL ON THE ALERT, OUR HERO HAS A *STRANGE FEELING* THAT ABBEY IS HIDING SOMEWHERE *IN THE CROWD*, THOUGH SHE MAY HAVE *CHANGED HER APPEARANCE...!*

Great Air Race Winner!
CONGRATULATIONS!

Bettie's Bonnets

1 x bespoke millinery item.

Paid for in full.

Please call again!

BB

① ITEM ONE: A RECEIPT

② ITEM TWO: A SMALL CASE

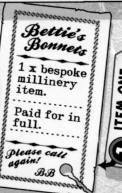

GLASSES
GLASSES

Effect on ...
Turns blon...
Turns blac...
Turns brow...

SUPER C...
AIR DY...
hair typ...
le hair ...
t hair b...
hair r...

COLOUR
...apte...
...ror...
...own...

③ ITEM THREE: BITS OF A BOX

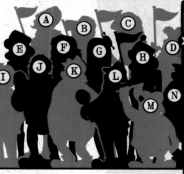

★ THE CHALLENGE! ★

LOOKING AT THE *ITEMS,* CAN YOU IDENTIFY *ABBEY* IN THE CROWD BEFORE SHE ESCAPES? WHAT IS HER LOCATION (A – N)?

ADVENTURE PROGRESS 97%

40

WITH *ABBEY* AND *KARMANN* SAFELY BEHIND BARS, VON DOOGAN RELAXES IN THE LUXURIOUS *HOWHI HOTEL*. FLICKING THROUGH THE PAPER, OUR HERO REALISES HE MAY HAVE UNCOVERED *MORE* THAN JUST SABOTEURS ON *MOUNT HOWHI!*

AH, A LITTLE BIT OF TIME TO LEAF THROUGH THE OLD *W.A.C.W.D.!* NOW, LET'S SEE ... HMM, IT SAYS THAT *ABBEY* AND *KARMANN* WERE *SISTERS!* I SHOULD HAVE SPOTTED THAT *SOONER!* AND WHAT ELSE ... HERE, WAIT A SEC! WHAT'S *THIS?!*

WORLD ADVENTURERS'
Weekly CLUB Digest

Vol. 26 — No. 13
(NEW SERIES.)

MELTING ICEBURG'S Strange LIFE FORMS – See Page 8

ASTEROID "X" CONTINUES TO *Baffle* SCIE—

THE GREAT AIR RACE

GREAT AIR RACE WINNER
Von Doogan was yesterday celebrating his victory in style with a large gathering of the world's press at the famous Mount Howhi Hotel. The intrepid aviator had beaten off fierce competition from seven of the world's great air men and women over the course of the long and arduous airborne adventure.

VON DOOGAN YESTERDAY

The race wasn't without its fair share of controversy, however, dogged as it was by sabotage from the very beginning. The first victim was the Oil Magnate Klaus Karr, who was poisoned at the first...

HOWHI MOUNTAIN RANGE CLAIMS ANOTHER VICTIM

VON DOOGAN'S AEROPLANE, the Thunderbolt, is the latest in a long line of aircraft to meet their end in the treacherous mountain pass. The air ace Milt Caniff lost his craft the Aero-DX5, Danny Dare crashed the legendary Anastasia-X, and F. Hampson bailed out of the Eagle Xero Special within the 20 mile mountain range.

SENSATIONAL ARREST!

MOMENTS AFTER WINNING the air race, Von Doogan pounced dramatically into the crowd of onlookers and pulled Abbey "Ace"...

WHITEOUT — HOWHI — SOLOW — CRAGGLE — THUNDERBOLT'S PATH

MOUNT HOWHI AND THE SURROUNDING PEAKS

THUNDERBOLT CRASH SITE

ABBEY IS KARMANN'S SISTER!

WINGS MUSEUM OPENING SOON

OWNER MR. R. WILSON tells us of two planes he has long hoped to discover for his collection: " The Old Blue Bomber, and of course Danny Dare's

THE CHALLENGE!

WHAT HAS DOOGAN DISCOVERED?

ADVENTURE COMPLETED!

THE CLUES

PUZZLE No. 1
REMEMBER, DOOGAN IS LOOKING AT THE TRAY FROM THIS SIDE...

PUZZLE No. 2
DOOGAN HAS FIGURED OUT THE *TOP ROW* OF NUMBERS:

PUZZLE No. 3
WHAT LINKS *THIS* COFFEE POT, AND *THE CIRCUS*?

PUZZLE No. 4
THESE ARE THE *FIRST FIVE TABLES*...

PUZZLE No. 5
AFTER THIS *PERSON BIDS*, THE TOTAL IS £14,150.

PUZZLE No. 6
ONE OF THE *KEYS* IS VERY *NEAR OUR HERO!*

PUZZLE No. 7
THIS PILOT FLIES ONE OF THESE PLANES...

PUZZLE No. 8
AVOID THE BOTTOM *TWO ROWS* OF SQUARES...

PUZZLE No. 9
THESE TWO PARTS ARE CLOSE TO EACH OTHER...

PUZZLE No. 10

DOOGAN WORKS OUT WHO SAT WHERE:

TOOLA
WINGNUT
MARLIN
DOOGAN
KARMANN
JAKOBS
KLAUS

1 2 A
3
4 5
B
6 7

PUZZLE No. 11
DOOGAN LOOKS UP...

PUZZLE No. 12

LOOK TO THE ___ WITH THE SKULLS. ___ IS NORTH-EAST OF ___

THIS PIECE GOES AT THE *TOP LEFT* OF THE RECTANGLE.

PUZZLE No. 13
DOOGAN DECODES ONE OF THE WORDS AS FOLLOWS:

STPMETTABALA = ATTEMPTS

PUZZLE No. 14
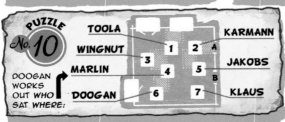

19

B BLOCK

YOU'RE ON THE RIGHT TRACK IF YOU USE *THIS* DOOR...

PUZZLE No. 15

EACH PLANE NEEDS *500 GALLONS* OF FUEL TO REACH CHECKPOINT 3...

PUZZLE No. 16
CHECKPOINT JIMJAM IS *NOT* IN EITHER OF THESE LOCATIONS:

PUZZLE No. 17
DOOGAN WILL NEED *FOUR* ITEMS FOR HIS ESCAPE ATTEMPT, THESE ARE *TWO* OF THEM...

PUZZLE No. 18
REMEMBER DOOGAN CAN MOVE LEFT OR RIGHT INTO A SQUARE HE'S OCCUPIED *BEFORE*. THIS WILL HELP YOU AVOID THE CLOUDS!

PUZZLE No. 19

DOOGAN HAS A SUDDEN BRAINWAVE...

TWO OF THESE CABLES DON'T LOOK QUITE RIGHT...!

PUZZLE No. 20

THIS MOUNTAIN MAY HELP YOU LOCATE ABBEY...

PUZZLE No. 21

DOOGAN WON'T BE HIRING ANY OF THESE TRUCKS...

PUZZLE No. 22

HERE ARE THE FIRST TWO CRATES IN PLACE...

PUZZLE No. 23

DOOGAN'S FIRST JOB IS TO LINK THE TWO ITEMS BELOW TOGETHER.

E → SOCKET 1

PUZZLE No. 24

FOLLOWING THE RULES CLOSELY IS ALL YOU NEED TO DO TO SOLVE THIS ONE.

PUZZLE No. 25

DOOGAN HAS CIRCLED TWO IMPORTANT BITS OF INFORMATION...

TRUCK LOAD CAPACITY
BIG RED............7 CRATES
LONG BACK............9 CRATES

TRUCK LOAD CAPACITY
THE LONG BOY............9 CRATES
WHITE 'UN............9 CRATES

PUZZLE No. 26

DOOGAN HAS SOLVED THE FIRST PUZZLE...

START: | STEP 1: PUSH "I" | STEP 2: PUSH "H" | STEP 3: PUSH "W"

PUZZLE No. 27

THINK ABOUT GENDER WHEN READING THE MESSAGE...

PUZZLE No. 28

DOOGAN FIRST JETTISONS...

...THIS MUCH FUEL...

...THIS MUCH WATER...

...PLUS HALF THE OIL. THESE ITEMS TOGETHER WEIGH 1,515LBS

PUZZLE No. 29

DOOGAN SUDDENLY SEES THAT TROUBLE IS CLOSER TO HIM THAN HE THOUGHT...!

PUZZLE No. 30

DOOGAN WORKS BACK FROM THIS FIRST TURN:

OPEN DOOR LOCK

PUZZLE No. 31

DOOGAN FINDS SOME MORE INFO ON THE PLANES:

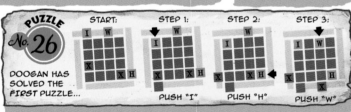

THE FIREFLY

CURRENT FORWARD SPEED:
75 METRES A SECOND
CURRENT DESCENT:
2.5 METRES A SECOND

THE THUNDERBOLT

CURRENT FORWARD SPEED:
100 METRES A SECOND
CURRENT DESCENT:
5 METRES A SECOND

PUZZLE No. 32

DOOGAN NEEDS TO REACH THREE BATTERIES...

PUZZLE No. 33

THESE THREE MOUNTAINS...

...APPEAR HERE ON THE MAP.

PUZZLE No. 34

DOOGAN USES EIGHT EXTINGUISHERS IN TOTAL, IN THE PICTURE ABOVE YOU CAN SEE FIVE OF THEM...

PUZZLE No. 35

CHALLENGE 1: THIS SIGN IS TRUE. → DOOR A IS NOT THE EXIT

CHALLENGE 2: THE DEACTIVATION PANEL CAN BE SEEN IN VIEW Y:

PUZZLE No. 36

DOOGAN PIECES THE BOX BITS TOGETHER...

SUPER COLOUR HAIR DYE:
Effect on hair types:
Turns blonde hair brown
Turns black hair blonde
Turns brown hair red

PUZZLE No. 37

THIS IS IT! AT LAST!

THE FINAL CHALLENGE! AND YOU KNOW WHAT? I THINK YOU'VE GOT WHAT IT TAKES TO SOLVE THIS ONE WITHOUT ANY HELP!

THE SOLUTIONS

PUZZLE 1 SANDWICH SECRET

1: THE MESSAGE READS:
"IN THE BLUE VASE ON THE SHELF."
2: DOOGAN SHOULD LOOK IN LOCATION **NINE**.

PUZZLE 3 AEROPLANE EXPENSE

1: DOOGAN NOTICES A *NEWSPAPER ARTICLE* IN PANEL THREE SAYING THAT A *LOCAL CIRCUS* HAS CLOSED. HE ALSO SEES THE *HUMAN CANNONBALL* FROM THE CIRCUS LOOKING FOR WORK IN PANEL TWO. SEEING A POSTER SAYING THAT THE CIRCUS DAREDEVIL PILOT SHOW HAS BEEN CANCELLED IN PANEL FOUR, DOOGAN WONDERS IF THE CIRCUS PILOT MAY BE LOOKING FOR WORK TOO. NOTICING THE *TATTOO* ON THE HAND OF THE PILOT IN THE POSTER, DOOGAN REALISES THAT *ABBEY "ACE" PONTOON* IS WORKING IN *THE CAFÉ IN PANEL FIVE.*
2: ALL THE ADVERTS FOR PLANES FOR SALE ARE EITHER *TOO EXPENSIVE*, OR *UNSUITABLE* FOR DOOGAN'S NEEDS. HOWEVER, A SIGN IN PANEL TWO AND A MESSAGE IN PANEL FOUR MAKE HIM THINK THAT HE MAY BE ABLE TO PICK UP A BARGAIN AT THE...
AIRFORCE SURPLUS AUCTION ON SATURDAY.

PUZZLE 5 THE BIDDING WAR

1: DOOGAN'S WINNING BID IS **£20,150**
2: HE HAS **£250** TO SPEND ON SUPPLIES.
3: DOOGAN SHOULD BUY:
THE DELUXE HAMPER,
THE TUBE-O-TRON RADIO,
THE BIG DROPPERS PARACHUTE SET
AND **THE FULL SET OF MAPS.**
4: THIS WILL LEAVE HIM WITH **£12.**

PUZZLE 2 THE MAGIC SQUARE

DOOGAN SOLVES THE *MAGIC SQUARE* PUZZLE SO THAT THE NUMBERS (READING LEFT TO RIGHT, TOP TO BOTTOM) ARE 4, 9, 2, 3, 5, 7, 8, 1, 6.
1: WITH THE *MAGIC SQUARE* FILLED IN, HE CAN DECODE MESSAGE "A", WHICH READS:
"THE RACE BEGINS AT BARLEY AIRFIELD"

2: DOOGAN DRAWS THE *TWO SQUARES* WITHIN THE *MAGIC SQUARE* LIKE THIS:

DOOGAN SEES THAT THE *CENTRE CIRCLE* IS IN A SQUARE, WHEREAS ALL THE OTHER EIGHT CIRCLES ARE ENCLOSED IN TRIANGLES. SO THE MESSAGE WILL SAY:
"THE RACE STARTS ON THE 5TH OF NOVEMBER"

PUZZLE 4 THE BIG COFFEE POT

USING THE *ROUTE* SHOWN ON THE *RIGHT*, DOOGAN'S *COFFEE POT* CALCULATION IS AS FOLLOWS:
7 − 2 − 3 − 1 − 1 + 3 − 2 − 1 + 5 − 3 − 1 − 1 + 5 − 4 − 1 + 3 − 1
THIS LEAVES DOOGAN WITH *TWO CUPS OF COFFEE* IN HIS POT AT THE *FINISH.*

PUZZLE 6 NAME THE PLANE

DOOGAN SHOULD NAME THE PLANE *"THE THUNDERBOLT".*

PUZZLE 7 RACE DAY!

SKY KING BELONGS TO *MARLIN*
CLOUD HOPPER BELONGS TO *TOOLA*
BARRACUDA BELONGS TO *JAKOBS*
SECRET WING BELONGS TO *WINGNUT*
ROYAL ROCKET BELONGS TO *GOUDA*
FIREFLY BELONGS TO *KARMANN*
CLUNKER BELONGS TO *KLAUS*

PUZZLE 8 TERRIFYING TAKE-OFF

DODGING AND WEAVING THROUGH THE ROUTE SHOWN ON THE *RIGHT*, DOOGAN WILL REACH *SAFE SQUARE ONE.*

PUZZLE 9 PERILOUS PART SWAP

DOOGAN NEEDS PARTS **8, 10 AND 23** TO FIX THE LANDING GEAR.

PUZZLE 10 THE BIG CHOKE

BY STUDYING THE EVIDENCE, DOOGAN SEES THAT...
GOUDA DIDN'T GO TO THE RESTAURANT.
MARLIN HAD A CHANCE TO POISON KLAUS'S STARTER.
KARMANN HAD A CHANCE TO POISON KLAUS'S DRINK.
TOOLA HAD A CHANCE TO POISON KLAUS'S STARTER AND HIS MAIN COURSE.
WINGNUT HAD A CHANCE TO POISON KLAUS'S STARTER.
EVEN *DOOGAN* HIMSELF HAD A CHANCE TO POISON KLAUS'S DESSERT.

ALL OF WHICH MEANS THAT THE *ONLY PILOT* WHO *DIDN'T* HAVE A CHANCE TO POISON KLAUS WAS *JAKOBS!*

PUZZLE 11 THE DEADLY OVERSLEEP

DOOGAN CAN USE THE *LADDER* TO REACH *SKYLIGHT B* AND THE *SCREWDRIVER* TO OPEN IT.

PUZZLE 12 SIX SCRAPS AND A MAP

THERE IS ONLY *ONE* RECTANGULAR CONFIGURATION OF THE SCRAPS IN WHICH *ALL THE DIRECTIONS* WILL LEAD DOOGAN TO A *SINGLE LOCATION* ON THE MAP. IN THIS CORRECT CONFIGURATION THE MESSAGE WILL READ:
"LOOK TO THE EAST OF THE ROCK WITH THE SKULLS. THE SHIPWRECK IS NORTH-EAST OF YOUR DESTINATION. YOUR GOAL IS SOUTH OF THE ROCK WITH THE LIGHTNING AND THE TREES NUMBERING NO MORE THAN THREE. YOUR DESTINATION IS NORTH OF THE REEF WITH THE SHARKS. WEST OF THE RED ISLAND YOU WILL FIND YOUR GOAL."
LOOKING AT THE MAP, DOOGAN SEES THAT THESE DIRECTIONS POINT TO *D2* AS THE DESTINATION.

PUZZLE 13 MIXED MESSAGES

CODE TYPE 6 AND *CODE TYPE 2* HAVE BEEN USED TOGETHER TO SCRAMBLE THE MESSAGE, WHICH WHEN UNSCRAMBLED READS:
"ATTEMPTS ON KLAUS AND WINGNUT SUCCESSFUL. HOWEVER VON DOOGAN ESCAPED. HE IS ON TO US. THINK WE MAY NEED TO MOVE TO PLAN TWO. GET THINGS READY ON THE AIRCRAFT CARRIER AND I WILL CONTACT YOU AGAIN IN TWO DAYS."

PUZZLE 14 FUEL FRENZY

THE CORRECT DOOR ORDER IS:
1 – 8 – 3 – 19 –
20 – 9 – 6 – 26

PUZZLE 16 THE CODED BOX

1: THE ROUTE CODE READS:
"GO UP TO DEAD MANS COVE. TURN LEFT AT CRAB ROCK. GO TO SHIP WITH NO SAIL. TURN UP BONE PASS THEN LAND AT PORT."
2: CHECKPOINT JIMJAM IS *LOCATION A*

PUZZLE 17 THE DREADED FOG

THE *ONLY OPTION* AVAILABLE TO DOOGAN THAT DOES NOT INVOLVE CRASHING THE PLANE IS TO TAKE THE PARACHUTE, MAP, COMPASS AND FLARES, AND THEN *PARACHUTE DOWN AND LIGHT FLARES* FOR ABBEY TO LAND BY.

PUZZLE 15 TANGLED TROUBLE

1: 50 BARRELS
2: 12,500 LITRES
3: 2,500 GALLONS
4: 5 PLANES
5: *JAKOBS'* LINE WILL BE KNOTTED, SO HE'LL BE LEFT *WITHOUT FUEL!*

PUZZLE 18 THE BIG JUMP

DOOGAN PARACHUTES DOWN THE ROUTE ON THE *RIGHT*, AND LANDS SAFELY IN *GROUND SQUARE D.*

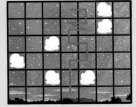

PUZZLE 19 CROSSED WIRES

STUDYING THE *WIRING DIAGRAMS*, DOOGAN SEES THAT THE *THIRD DIAGRAM FROM THE LEFT* IS THE MOST SIMILAR TO THE *CONTROL DESK*. HE REALISES THAT IF HE *UNPLUGS THE CABLE FROM SOCKET 6 AND PLUGS IT IN TO SOCKET 10*, AND THEN *REMOVES THE CABLE THAT RUNS FROM SOCKET 1 TO SOCKET 9*, HE'LL HAVE THE CONTROL DESK WORKING AGAIN!

PUZZLE 20 SPLASH DOWN

1: DOOGAN SHOULD SEND THE LIFEBOAT TO *D3.*
2: TOOLA IS 5,000FT UP, SO WHEN SHE JUMPS, THE FIRST 1,000FT OF FREEFALL WILL TAKE 10 SECONDS, THE SECOND 1,000FT WILL TAKE 5 SECONDS, THEN SHE'LL OPEN HER PARACHUTE AND WILL DROP THE REMAINING 3,000FT AT 15FT PER SECOND, WHICH WILL TAKE 200 SECONDS. THE WATER WILL BE FREEZING, MEANING SHE WILL LAST 7 MINUTES IN THE OCEAN ONCE SHE HITS. SO, ALTOGETHER THEY HAVE *10 MINUTES AND 35 SECONDS* TO SAVE HER!

PUZZLE 21 PICK-A-TRUCK

THE FASTEST TWO TRUCKS THAT CAN PULL THE FULL WEIGHT OF THE THUNDERBOLT ARE *TRUCKS 2 AND 4: BIG RED AND THE LONG BOY.*

PUZZLE 23 A RIFT IN THE DRIFT

THE HEATERS SHOULD BE *PLUGGED IN* AND *PLACED* AS FOLLOWS:
*MAMMOTH BLOWER 1 –
LOCATION: J   SOCKET: 3
MAMMOTH BLOWER 2 –
LOCATION: I   SOCKET: 2
MOUSE BLOWER –
LOCATION: E   SOCKET: 1*

PUZZLE 24 BOULDER OF DOOM

AFTER SIX MOVES, *GOUDA'S* TRUCK WILL GET HIT BY THE BOULDER, ALL THE OTHER RACERS ESCAPE *UNHARMED!*

PUZZLE 22 A HEAVY LOAD

WITH THE CRATES ARRANGED IN THE CORRECT ORDER, AS SHOWN BELOW, THE MESSAGE READS:
"SNOW DRIFT AHEAD!"

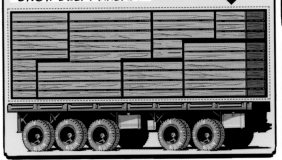

PUZZLE 25 THE MISSING CRATE MYSTERY

1: DOOGAN STUDIES THE *TRUCK LOAD CAPACITIES* AND REALISES THAT ONLY THE *FIREFLY'S* TRUCKS HAVE THE CAPACITY TO HOLD TWO EXTRA CRATES.
2: AS THE CRATES ARE LABELLED ALPHABETICALLY, AND DOOGAN CAN SEE THAT THE FIRST 16 CRATES (LABELLED A – P) WERE *CORRECTLY* DELIVERED TO BARNEY POOCHE, THE THUNDERBOLT'S HAULING TRUCK TEAM LEADER, THEN THE MISSING TWO CRATES MUST BE *Q* AND *R.*

PUZZLE 26 THE FINAL DESTINATION

READ BACKWARDS, THE CODE SAYS: *"FLY TO MOUNT HOWHI"*

PUZZLE 27 FLAG FLUMMOX

THE MESSAGE READS: "THE WING SUPPORTS HAVE BEEN WEAKENED. HE WILL CRASH ON TAKEOFF". AS DOOGAN'S PLANE IS SAFE, "HE" MUST REFER TO ... **MARLIN!**

PUZZLE 28 DEAD WEIGHT

THE FIRST THINGS DOOGAN JETTISONS ARE ALL THE *TOOL KITS* (TOTAL WEIGHT 408 LBS), THE SPARE PARTS (TOTAL WEIGHT: 750 LBS) AND THE HANG GLIDER (127 LBS). THESE ITEMS COMBINED LIGHTEN THE THUNDERBOLT BY 1,285 LBS. DOOGAN THEN CALCULATES THAT THE THUNDERBOLT WILL NEED 300 GALLONS OF *FUEL*, 30 GALLONS OF *WATER* AND 30 GALLONS OF *OIL* TO MAKE IT TO *MOUNT HOWHI*. THIS MEANS HE CAN JETTISON 200 GALLONS OF *FUEL*, 10 GALLONS OF *WATER*, AND 30 GALLONS OF *OIL*. USING THE LIQUID WEIGHTS CONVERSION CHART, DOOGAN WORKS OUT THAT THIS COMES TO A TOTAL OF 1,515 LBS.

1: USING THE ABOVE CALCULATION, WE CAN SEE THAT WITH THE *TOOL KITS*, SPARE PARTS, UNWANTED FUEL, OIL AND WATER JETTISONED, THE THUNDERBOLT IS **2,800 LBS** LIGHTER.

2: THE THUNDERBOLT'S SPEED HAD BEEN 250MPH, BUT IT BECOMES FASTER BY 1MPH FOR EVERY 140 LBS OF WEIGHT IT LOOSES THIS MEANS THAT ONCE DOOGAN HAS JETTISONED ALL 2,800 LBS OF DEAD WEIGHT, THE PLANE WILL BE TRAVELLING 20MPH FASTER, MAKING ITS NEW SPEED **170MPH.**

PUZZLE 29 THE BIG GIVEAWAY

ALL THE *EVIDENCE* AND *INCIDENTS* LEAD OUR HERO TO *ONE CONCLUSION:*
"DOOGAN HAS REALISED THAT FROM THE VERY BEGINNING, THE *SABOTAGE* OF THE OTHER RACERS, AND THE ATTEMPTS TO FORCE *HIM* OUT OF THE RACE, HAVE BEEN CARRIED OUT BY KARMANN AND **ABBEY!**"

PUZZLE 30 COCKPIT LOCKOUT

TO OPEN THE DOOR (AND *NOT* BLOW HIMSELF UP!), DOOGAN SHOULD TURN THE CRANK ANTI-CLOCKWISE, TOWARDS **"A".**

PUZZLE 31 MID-AIR MELTDOWN

1: THE FIREFLY IS *TRAVELLING FORWARDS* AT 75 METRES PER SECOND, AND *DESCENDING* AT 2.5 METRES PER SECOND.

2: THE THUNDERBOLT IS *TRAVELLING FORWARDS* AT **100** METRES PER SECOND, AND *DESCENDING* AT 5 METRES PER SECOND.

3: AFTER 12 SECONDS, THE *FIREFLY* WILL BE IN **P3** AND THE *THUNDERBOLT* WILL BE IN **P5**.

4: THE *FIREFLY* WILL BE 20 METRES BELOW THE *THUNDERBOLT*, GIVING DOOGAN A **50%** CHANCE!

PUZZLE 32 MID-AIR BREAK-IN

TO GET TO THE COCKPIT *WITHOUT* SETTING AN ALARM OFF DOOGAN MUST FIRST REACH THROUGH **WINDOW B** AND REMOVE **BATTERY 2**. HE CAN THEN ENTER THE PLANE THROUGH **HATCH C**. NEXT HE MUST REMOVE **BATTERY 1** WHICH WILL ALLOW HIM TO GO THROUGH **DOOR H**...

...FINALLY HE MUST *CRAWL* THROUGH TO **BATTERY 4** AND REMOVE IT, SO THAT HE CAN ENTER THE *COCKPIT* THROUGH **DOOR I** AND CATCH KARMANN *UNAWARES.*

PUZZLE 33 HUNT FOR HOWHI

1: THE FIREFLY IS IN **B4**.

2: DOOGAN SHOULD FLY **NORTH**.

PUZZLE 34 BLAZING MAZE

DOOGAN FOLLOWS THE ROUTE SHOWN HERE...

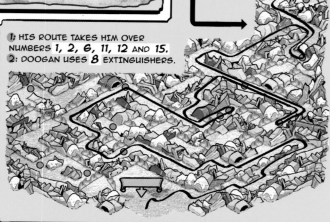

PUZZLE 35 DUPLICITOUS DOORS

1: ONLY *ONE* OF THE SIGNS ON THE DOORS CAN BE *TRUE*. THE SIGN ON *DOOR A* CAN'T BE TRUE, BECAUSE THAT WOULD MEANT DOOR B'S SIGN WOULD *ALSO* BE TRUE, AND VICE VERSA. SO, THE SIGN ON *DOOR C* MUST BE *TRUE*, MEANING THE SIGNS ON DOORS A AND B ARE *LIES*. THIS TELLS DOOGAN THAT **DOOR B** IS THE EXIT.

2: DOOGAN SHOULD PRESS THE **GREEN** PANEL TO *DEACTIVATE* THE CUBE BOMB.

3: THE LETTERS A – I ARE REPRESENTED BY THE FOLLOWING NUMBERS: A = 3 B = 1 C = 4 D = 7 E = 5 F = 6 G = 2 H = 8 I = 9, SO DOOGAN SHOULD ENTER:
3, 1, 4, 7, 5, 6, 2, 8, 9.

1: HIS ROUTE TAKES HIM OVER NUMBERS 1, 2, 6, 11, 12 AND 15.

2: DOOGAN USES **8** EXTINGUISHERS.

PUZZLE 36 THE BIG PARTY

DOOGAN KNOWS THAT ABBEY IS WEARING A HAT AND GLASSES, AND THAT THE "SUPER COLOUR HAIR DYE" WILL HAVE TURNED HER BROWN HAIR RED. THIS DESCRIPTION FITS THE PERSON IN LOCATION **H**, SO THAT MUST BE ABBEY!

PUZZLE 37 DOOGAN'S DISCOVERY

DOOGAN HAS DISCOVERED THE LOCATION OF THE LOST **ANASTASIA-X** PLANE FLOWN BY **DANNY DARE!** IT'S IN THE BACKGROUND OF THE *THUNDERBOLT CRASH SITE* PHOTO!

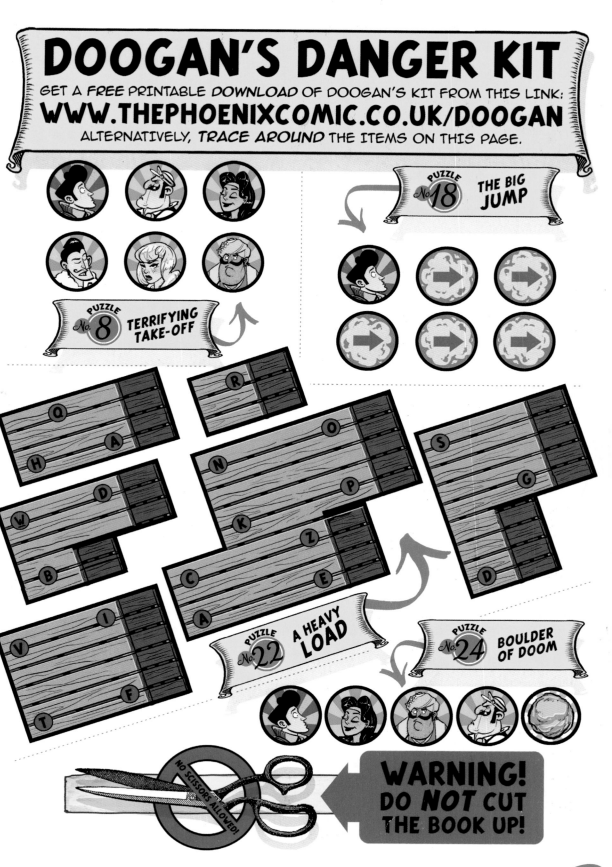

This book is dedicated to my brother, Robin Etherington.

Thank you for tirelessly play-testing every puzzle, game, and invention I've ever come up with from the cardboard computers I made when I was eight, to the book you now hold in your hands.

I feel incredibly lucky to have illustrated your wonderful stories, and then taken those stories on tour around the world with you.

I love you, bro!

VON DOOGAN AND THE GREAT AIR RACE
is
A DAVID FICKLING BOOK

First published in Great Britain in 2016 by
David Fickling Books,
31 Beaumont Street,
Oxford, OX1 2NP

www.davidficklingbooks.com

Text and illustrations © Lorenzo Etherington, 2016

978-1-910200-82-7

1 3 5 7 9 10 8 6 4 2

The right of Lorenzo Etherington to be identified as the author and illustrator of this work has been asserted in accordance with the Copyright, Designs and Patents Act 1988.

DAVID FICKLING BOOKS Reg. No. 8340307

A CIP catalogue record for this book is available from the British Library.

Printed and bound in Great Britain by Polestar Stones.

David Fickling Books supports the Forest Stewardship Council (FSC), the leading international forest certification organisation. All our titles that are printed on Greenpeace-approved FSC-certified paper carry the FSC logo.

FSC
www.fsc.org
MIX
Paper from
responsible sources
FSC® C020872